In Memory

This book is in fond memory of Jonathan Eshenour,
one of my very favorite little friends.
Jonathan not only kept me on my toes,
he kept me supplied with smiles.
In his life as well as his passing,
Jonathan elevated his brother,
Matthew, to the role of hero.
Thank you, Jonathan, for the lessons you taught me.

ALSO BY GRETCHEN GOODMAN

I Can Learn! Strategies and Activities for Gray-Area Children

Inclusive Classrooms from A to Z: A Handbook for Educators

Classroom Strategies for "Gray-Area" Children (video)

For more information on attending a workshop with Gretchen Goodman, or having her come to your school for an inservice seminar, contact:

The Society For Developmental Education
Ten Sharon Road, PO Box 577
Peterborough, NH 03458
1-800-924-9621

MORE I Can Learn!

Strategies and Activities for Gray-Area Children

Gretchen Goodman

Published by
Crystal Springs Books • Peterborough, New Hampshire
1-800-321-0401

Printed in the United States of America
09 08 07 06 05 8 7 6 5 4

Published and Distributed by:

Crystal Springs Books
Ten Sharon Road, Box 500
Peterborough, NH 03458-0500
800-321-0401

Publisher Cataloging-in-Publication Data

Goodman, Gretchen, 1952- ,
More I Can Learn! / by Gretchen Goodman ; illustrated by Susan Dunholter.—1st. ed.
[171]p. : Ill. ; cm.
Includes bibliographic references.
Summary: This sequel to "I Can Learn! Strategies and Activities for Gray-Area Children" includes more ideas for adapting math, reading, writing, and spelling activities for struggling learners. Includes areas to help parents help their children learn.
ISBN 1-884548-18-0
1. Learning, disabled children—Education (Elementary)—United States. 2. Education, Elementary—Activity programs—United States. I. Dunholter, Susan, ill. II. Title.
371-91 —dc21 1997 CIP
LC Card Number: 97-77086

Design and illustrations: Susan Dunholter
Editor: Aldene Fredenburg

Dedication

This book is lovingly dedicated to my mother and father, who are the kind of parents with whom all educators wish they could work on a daily basis. Thank you for never clipping my wings, but always making me accountable for my actions. I am proud to call you Mom and Dad.

This book is also dedicated to my buddy, Tyler Simons, and his mom, JoDell — you remind me daily how the gift of love can conquer any challenge.

Acknowledgments

Thanks to my favorite PR person and supporter, Harry. He never stops cheering me on;

A special "I love you" to my daughter, Aimee, who is the light of my life and my best friend;

An extra bone and pull toy for my writing companion, Bubba, who lies faithfully on my feet while I write, whether it be at 2:00 a.m. or 8:00 p.m.;

To my many friends and colleagues at SDE, thank you for all the doors you have opened for me and the many opportunities you've given me;

To my talented editor, Aldene Fredenburg — I appreciate how your expertise has kept me focused and organized;

And to my mentor, Jim Grant, thank you for being such a wonderful teacher and friend. Your caring and giving attitude has taught me the true meaning of life.

Contents

Preface

Children today are very different from children of even five years ago. More and more of them are recognized as having learning difficulties; their self-esteem is more fragile than ever; many are living in families headed either by a single parent or by two working parents who have little free time to focus on their children's educational or social needs.

At the same time children's needs are increasing, budget cuts are threatening the services that meet those needs. More and more school districts are limiting special education services to those children most severely affected. This means that the "tweeners" or gray-area children, those who need just a little bit of help, are less likely to get that help.

"Somehow, among all these pressures and all these demands, children still need to develop basic skills."

In the midst of all this, everyone's expectations have been raised. Children used to TVs, VCRs, cellular phones, computers and Gameboys demand high-interest activities rather than the "skill and drill" methods of a decade ago. Teachers are faced with a curriculum that demands more of students at an earlier age. Society's reliance on technology demands that students become proficient at that technology.

Somehow, among all these pressures and all these demands, children still need to develop basic skills; and children who are struggling need extra help with those skills.

When I published my book, *I Can Learn! Strategies and Activities for Gray-Area Children*, I was amazed at the response. Teachers from all over the country not only bought the book, but asked for more activities to help them help the struggling learners in their classrooms. *More I Can Learn!* is the response to that request. It provides the primary teacher with easy-to-use, fun, creative activities that specifically address the difficulties children have in learning. While these activities are designed to help struggling learners, they are suitable for all children, and will be enjoyed by all children.

I thank the many teachers who have shared their successful strategies with me and other participants in my seminars; it is because of them that children across the country can say, and truly believe, that "I Can Learn!"

How to Use This Book

More I Can Learn is organized by specific areas of the curriculum and can be used by classroom teachers, parents, teaching assistants, peer tutors and specialists. I advise readers to observe and assess children carefully and develop programs to meet individual needs.

Try several ideas in each section, document what you've tried, and if you discover other successful adaptations, jot down your ideas in the margins. What you learn in working with one child may help another child later on.

Activities particularly well suited for students who learn through auditory, kinesthetic, tactile, or visual modalities will be marked by the following symbols in the margins:

Meaningful hands-on experiences can help all students reach their full learning potential.

= auditory

= visual

= tactile

= kinesthetic

Activities that are particularly good to use with partners, cooperative learning groups, or small groups are also noted.

= partners

= cooperative learning
(may be partners or groups)

= small groups

No activity in this book is only for the at-risk learner. Meaningful hands-on experiences can help all students reach their full learning potential.

Questions and Answers About Struggling Learners

In my conferences and customized trainings, I meet teachers who ask numerous questions about struggling learners. Often called "gray-area children," "tweeners," and "crackers," these students are in danger of falling between the cracks if they don't receive the modifications and adaptations they need in the classroom.

Here are answers to the twenty questions teachers ask most often about these children — who they are, what characteristics they have, and how we can meet their needs.

1 What is a struggling learner?

A struggling learner is a student who has difficulty keeping up with classmates of the same age in a developmentally appropriate learning environment.

The struggling learner does not qualify for special education services, or in many cases for remedial or other school services. Whereas the learning disabled child has peaks and valleys in knowledge and skill levels, often the struggling learner's strengths and needs can be described as "flat." Struggling learners often:

- have difficulty organizing themselves and their work environment.
- do not take oral directions the first time given.
- are overwhelmed by work tasks and need work chunked for them.
- have weak social and emotional skills.

These children can easily fall between the cracks of the educational system unless we provide them with the assistance they need.

2

Why are classroom teachers faced with an increasing number of struggling learners?

Today's classrooms reflect society. In this country we are dealing with young mothers, in both urban and rural areas, with inadequate prenatal care — which often results in premature, low birthweight babies. We have young parents who used alcohol and drugs during pregnancy. We have children being placed in inadequate child care facilities, or who are being cared for by teen mothers as young as fourteen. Additionally, many children are being raised in single-parent homes, or in homes where both parents may work several jobs, leaving little time for the children.

These children suffer on two fronts: their environment is lacking in the support and stimulation that allows them to learn some of the basic knowledge they need in order to succeed in school; and the energy required to survive in poverty, in stressful, sometimes dysfunctional home environments, robs children of the focus and concentration they need in the classroom.

Of course, not all struggling learners come from poverty or neglect, or from stressful homes. Many children are struggling in school because their natural learning patterns do not fit the learning structure of the classroom.

3 Will a summer school program cure these children?

Summer school programs can certainly help maintain a continuum for these children, so that they can progress at their own rate, retain knowledge from the previous year, and avoid losing ground over the summer. If a child is lagging only slightly behind his class, he may enter school in the fall more on a par with the other children.

However, a summer program can't accelerate the child's normal learning process, and if a child is a year behind the rest of his class, he is certainly not going to catch up to the other students in two or three months' time. The child who does catch up in September may start to lag behind again as the year progresses, because he is operating within his *normal learning pace.*

It is important to recognize that struggling learners *do not need to be cured.* Rather, they need material presented to them in a variety of ways, and in small chunks; and they need to be able to work in ways that show what they know while adapting to their special circumstances.

4

Is retention a viable option for the struggling learner?

Retention is appropriate for some children under some circumstances, but is usually *not* a good option for the struggling learner. Retention works best for children who are bright, but developmentally young; the extra year allows them to be placed in a classroom of students who are at the same age developmentally, and to catch up to grade level during the extra year.

Struggling learners, on the other hand, are working at their natural capacity. They will not rise to the top of their class with an extra year, but will continue to struggle as their classmates move on, because there is a disparity in their skill level and ability to learn compared with their "regular" classmates. All the extra time in the world will not change that.

A teacher who is faced with the decision of retaining a student should seek the guidance of a professional support team; this is not a decision that should be made independently. The team should evaluate the child and determine, among other things, whether the child is truly a slow learner or just developmentally young.

In ideal circumstances, the support team should include the teacher about to receive the struggling student. Once the team determines that the child is a slow learner, it can discuss as a group interventions and adaptations that will help the student succeed in the new grade.

5 Why not just put these students into special classes?

Very often these children don't meet the guidelines set up by school districts for special education services. Need for these services is determined by a combination of standardized assessment tools, such as IQ tests, and evaluation of a child's classroom performance. Many gray-area children are working within their ability range, which falls outside of the mandated criteria for special education or learning disabled status.

Learning-disabled children may have an IQ of 131 in verbal ability but an overall performance score of 91; this discrepancy between ability and classroom achievement could qualify them for support services. Struggling learners, on the other hand, may test at a straight across-the-board IQ of 80 to 89, and be performing at that level in the classroom—which could preclude their getting special services.

6 How can I ever teach to all the different ability levels within my classroom?

Many of the teaching strategies that work so well in today's classrooms are of special benefit to struggling learners — and to the teacher who has to attend to the diverse needs of his or her students. These methods help optimize the learning and teaching environment in a diverse classroom:

- Use flexible grouping; have children work in whole group, small groups, with partners, and individually as needed. Team-teaching arrangements, wise use of aides, and "push in" arrangements in which special education personnel and other specialists come into the classroom and work with the classroom teacher, are great ways of optimizing flexible grouping strategies.
- Use thematic learning, building lessons around key topics and ideas. This serves to integrate the curriculum and to heighten the children's interest levels.
- Include topics chosen by students in the curriculum; allow students to choose *how* some topics will be studied.
- Create a peer tutoring program within the classroom, so students can help each other learn.
- Create a cross-age tutoring program to give younger students role models and to give older students the opportunity to *be* role models.
- Utilize senior citizen volunteers as teacher aides or as special guests to present interesting topics to children. Some school districts have created programs for senior citizens who receive a tax break in exchange for volunteering in the schools.
- Use cooperative learning strategies.

It's interesting to note that many of the instructional strategies which benefit struggling learners involve interpersonal relationships, either with other students or with a caring adult. Probably the single most important factor in motivating struggling learners is support and acceptance from the people in their lives.

Are there adaptations I can make in my teaching without changing a lot of the materials?

Yes, there are many things you can do:

- Begin by teaching in a variety of modalities. Most teachers have been taught in a combination auditory and visual style, listening to a college professor lecture in front of a large class while the professor writes information on a blackboard. We tend to carry that method of teaching into our classrooms. Unfortunately, struggling learners seldom learn well in a strictly auditory or visual manner, but need other methods, including tactile/kinesthetic experiences and a lot of interpersonal activities.
- Break the students' work into small, bite-size pieces. Instead of assigning a whole chapter on Monday to be completed by Friday, assign the student six to eight pages a night.
- Have a study buddy assigned to every student. The struggling learner can share study notes and call her study buddy with homework questions.
- Have materials and lessons taped for students. This will allow struggling readers to keep up with the class in terms of content. The student can also use the tapes to help follow along with written material.
- Give students plenty of breaks throughout the day. A break could be something as simple as walking to the office for supplies, feeding a class pet, or collecting papers.

8 Are these adaptations only used for the gray-area child?

Absolutely not! It is amazing how many teachers contact me after workshops and inservices to share the successes they've had with *all* children using some of the *I Can Learn* activities and adaptations. What makes a struggling learner's life simpler can often help ease learning for children not considered struggling. These adaptations can become a natural part of the teacher's bag of tricks in dealing with all students on a daily basis.

How can I help gray-area learners organize themselves and their materials?

It would be wonderful if parents taught young children the basics of organization: where to keep their toys and clothes, how to clean up after themselves, etc. Unfortunately, most children come to school without these skills. School is usually the first time the child is expected to be organized, so you have your work cut out for you. Here are some tips which are helpful for all students, but particularly for the struggling learner:

- Have a laminated "To Do" list on the child's desk. This will help the child organize his time.
- Have the child list the day's activities, then check off each item as it is completed.
- Have the student keep materials in the same location each day — a cubby, mailbox, chair pack, or desk.
- Teach the student to make a desk map to help organize the materials inside.
- Color-code book covers by subject, and have matching color-coded notebooks for the student — red for math, blue for writing, for instance.
- Use a parent letter or assignment book to keep parents informed of upcoming events and requirements. If necessary, ask the parent to sign the assignment book each night (after checking to see that the assignment has been completed) and return the book to the school with the student the following day.
- At the end of each week, send home a summary sheet tallying work completed, test or paper scores, and class participation.

What do I tell other students who say, "It's not fair that Johnny gets to do it a special way"?

10

It is our role as classroom teachers to communicate to students that we all have our strengths and needs in life. Some of us can do cursive writing, others excel with printing. Some students can play baseball, others hockey. Most importantly, we need to get across the idea that "fair" doesn't mean that everyone gets the same things in life; it means that everyone gets what he or she needs in order to succeed in life.

At the same time, try to avoid having struggling learners get too much special treatment. When one student uses a fun adaptation such as Post-It note writing, let other students try it too. If a student gets to do an oral book report rather than a written one, provide that option for other students as well, at least some of the time. Once in a while, give a test and allow all students to circle the ten questions they want to answer on the test.

Most importantly, we need to model behavior for students by presenting ourselves as individuals who struggle and ask for help in some areas, and excel in others.

11 How can we build self-esteem in the struggling learner?

When a child is struggling in school — when he can't grasp the material, when she sees herself falling behind her classmates, when parental anxiety (and sometimes pressure) rises at home — the struggling learner's self-esteem plummets. Building it up again is paramount.

The key is to discover and recognize the students' strengths outside the academic area:

- Struggling learners tend to be very empathetic with other learners, and often make outstanding helpers who eagerly assist the teacher with a variety of activities. Appoint them as wheelchair drivers and peer tutors to special-needs students. Let them assist in lower elementary grades and tutor younger students. Give them the opportunity to read to kindergarteners or tape-record books for other classes.
- These children often relate very strongly to class pets. Make sure they have an opportunity to care for these animals.
- Pay attention to the lives these children have outside the classroom. If Mark hit a softball and made a home run at recess, mention it in class.
- Encourage children to bring in hobbies and discuss them during a sharing time. If they know how to do something involved with their hobby, ask them to teach the rest of the class.
- Have all the children in the class make an "I Can" collage, helping them focus on activities with which they can succeed. Let the children in the classroom suggest skills and abilities to each other. ("Mark, you sure can hit a ball!")

12 Should I grade these students differently than other students in my room?

If a school district continues to grade and evaluate student progress with a standardized letter report card, classroom teachers need to document all modifications made for a struggling learner in order to assist next year's teacher. It is also important to document the adaptations and modifications made for a student for his parents, and to keep the parents well informed about the child's progress and the use of specific modifications. For instance:

- Has the teacher read all the tests to the child?
- Has the reading material been taped for the child?
- Have directions given orally to the class also been written for the child?
- Has the material been retaught in a variety of ways?

Many school districts attach a modification sheet to the child's report card to inform both the parents and next year's teacher of the modifications.

Schools who have begun to use anecdotal records, authentic assessment, and portfolios to evaluate students are likely to get a more accurate view of what their struggling learners can do.

Struggling learners may need *some* modifications in *some* areas, rather than across the curriculum. For instance, a child can compute mathematics problems, but can't do as many in the same amount of time as the average learner. Another student may find an oral book report easier to do than a written one. In both instances, the modifications show mastery of the subjects and skills that need to be measured.

When the amount of needed modifications for a particular child exceeds the amount of learning taking place, it may be necessary to provide the child with more individually designed instruction in the form of special education.

13 How should I handle test taking with my struggling learners?

Test taking needs to be modified for struggling learners, just as notetaking and projects are adapted. Here are some adaptations that can be used as needed:

- For students with reading difficulties, read the tests to them.
- Provide a study guide to help students study before the test.
- Give untimed tests to students who work more slowly than their classmates.
- Give tests in small chunks. Alternatively, tell children to work on the test for twenty minutes; they will be scored only on what they complete.
- Have children try the whole test, then circle the ten questions on which they want to be scored.
- Allow children to choose ten out of twenty spelling words when they are first assigned. The children understand that they can study these ten words, and will only be tested on these words.
- Alternatively, the students can take the entire test, but will only be scored on these ten words.
- Give students an open-book test or notebook test, where they can use their class work for assistance.
- Try giving struggling learners the first letter of each answer as a clue.
- Allow these students to use word banks or answer keys during tests.

14 How can I help parents better understand and support their child?

All parents want their children to succeed; when it becomes evident that a child is having difficulty in school, parents experience tremendous anxiety. It's important for the school to provide as much information as they can, as well as a lot of support, for these parents as they work with the school to help their child.

A child experiencing problems academically may have been informally evaluated by a classroom teacher, or the evaluation may have gone beyond that to some type of formalized assessment tools or even special education screening.

Whatever form the evaluation takes, parents need to be given a complete, accurate understanding of the results, and the steps the school plans to take to address the child's learning difficulties. Parents need to be told: "Here's what we think the difficulty is; here's what we plan to do about it; here's what we hope to accomplish."

It's important to explain to parents the curriculum, the classroom structure, and instructional strategies utilized on a day-to-day basis in their child's classroom. Parents may not understand concepts like invented spelling, thematic teaching, and cooperative learning, and may blame these unfamiliar strategies for their child's lack of success. Here are other ways to include parents:

- Make periodic phone calls to parents to let them know of their child's successes in the classroom.
- Show parents work samples from both typical learners and struggling learners, so they can understand the difference in work products and expectations between these two groups of children. Work samples can also provide a goal and some type of guide as their child works on particular skills.
- Invite parents to the classroom frequently, not just for report card conferences. Let them see how your classroom functions, and what the expectations for your class are in terms of learning and behavior.
- Give parents of struggling learners the opportunity to participate in student workshops and book groups; this will give them a chance to work with a variety of students and gain some perspective on their own child's learning patterns.
- Have a school fun night for families. This allows parents to see their children in school having a good time and interacting in a way that doesn't involve academics. (Sometimes, when a child is having trouble

in school, the school takes on an ominous presence for the entire family. Periodic, non-academic activities help to dispel this.)

- Videotape your classroom so that parents who can't break away from a job can see how the class functions on a daily basis, and how their own child functions within the class. (This is a valuable strategy for all parents; their children may act very differently when parents are in the classroom than they would ordinarily act.)
- Communicate with parents through communication logs, diaries, journals, and newsletters.
- Most importantly, encourage parents to attend all team meetings called to discuss modifications and supports implemented for their child in the classroom.

Be aware that many parents with struggling learners have been through numerous bouts of testing and evaluation of their children, sometimes with conflicting results, and many learning strategies may have been tried unsuccessfully. Parents will often come to you exhausted, confused, and frustrated at their inability to find answers for their child. You need to treat them with patience, respect, and kindness, and assure them that you're going to hang in there with them and their child.

Are there ways for parents to help these students at home?

15

There are many ways parents can help their children at home:

- Struggling learners often need to have material repeated at home, and need the chance to rehearse material. Teachers can help with this by providing parents with rehearsal calendars that tell the parents what subjects need to be reviewed. This gives the child the opportunity to acquire some basic knowledge about a subject before facing it in class.
- Parents must be included in all team meetings where interventions are being designed for the student.
- Send parents taped versions of books and oral classroom lectures so that they can review the material with the child.

If parent support is lacking in the home, it is the school's responsibility to provide the child with someone at school who can rehearse and review classroom material with the child. This person can be a paid teacher's aide, a high school volunteer, a PTO volunteer, or a mentor teacher from another classroom willing to volunteer time to help this student.

16 What happens when a child moves? I have worked so hard to develop adaptations for children, and I'm afraid the new teacher won't.

It's hard for us to accept that, when a child moves, we lose the ability to provide the help that we know the child needs. Concern over the capabilities of the child's next teacher is natural. We need to provide all the adaptations and modifications the child needs as long as she is in our care, and accept the fact that, once she is gone, there is not much we can do.

One thing we *can* do is document all the adaptations and modifications we have provided for the child, and include all specific adaptation and modification sheets we have used. Also send along a copy of any behavior management plan developed for the child. Make sure you let the new school's administration know that you will be willing to communicate personally with the new teacher and specialists in order to give them an understanding of how to help the child.

17 My principal expects all students to be "on level" at the end of the school year. How can I inform her of the improbability of this happening?

First of all, you need to ask for a definition of "on level." Does this mean that all children exiting from a single-year first grade will be reading materials designated for "end-of-year" first grade? This is not only unlikely, it is virtually impossible.

If your principal believes it is possible, you have a problem. You need to share information with the principal on your own periodic assessments of the students, showing where the students were academically at the beginning of the year compared where they are at the end of the year. Being able to show the students' progress throughout the year will help, and will (one hopes) give the principal an inkling of the normal variations in academic development among students.

Of course, this means you have to have your own assessment act together. Make sure you have plenty of work samples contained in your student portfolios that accurately show your students' progression in skills. In terms of your struggling learners, you will be able to show growth on a continuum, even though it may not be at a specific grade level. You can also periodically audio- and videotape children working and reading in the classroom to show growth.

Invite your principal into your classroom to participate in book sharing with the students; have her observe the students as they work in learning centers, and as you apply a variety of adaptations throughout the classroom. Give your principal the opportunity to interact on a personal level with your struggling students so that she can gain an understanding of how these children function.

18 What kind of training do I need to motivate and teach struggling learners?

Unfortunately, there is no one easy answer in terms of teaching struggling learners. Teachers need to take a patient, trial-and-error approach to discover what works with each student.

However, training in certain instructional strategies and educational concepts will give the classroom teacher valuable tools in dealing with these students. Teachers should consider training to enable them to do the following:

- Combine literature-based reading and writing instruction with more structured methods. Struggling learners *need* structure, but do not react well to isolated drills. Integrating structured lessons in phonics and other decoding skills with exciting children's literature will provide both the structure and the motivation these learners need.
- Teachers need to understand how to adapt instruction for children who learn differently. For instance, when learning the concept of addition, some students will be able to add the numbers mentally without use of manipulatives, some may place objects next to the numbers and count them, and others will regroup the numbers. The teacher needs to be able to teach these different approaches as appropriate for a particular student.
- Develop adaptations and modifications in classroom instruction and assignments appropriate to the students' needs.
- Create student-centered classrooms in which instruction is geared toward the students' ability levels and needs, rather than providing a ready-made curriculum and fitting the students into the curriculum. Develop a method by which students can have input into the curriculum and the classroom's rules of conduct.
- Create learning centers as part of the classroom environment.
- Develop cooperative learning opportunities.
- Develop an assessment program using portfolios and work samples.
- Adjust the pace and presentation of subject matter according to the varying needs of the children in the class.
- Develop collaborative teaching and planning strategies to provide support for each other as teachers.
- Apply constructivist learning and brain-based learning concepts to instruction, emphasizing learning as a process rather than a product.
- Design lessons to begin with concrete activities and then move to abstract concepts.

19 How can I get support for myself within the school setting?

Some years ago, a teacher's only option in getting support was to refer the struggling learner to a child study team, which essentially meant the team would *test the child.*

There is a better way. Instead of sending the child down the hall to be tested, many schools are setting up strong building-based assistance teams which provide instructional support for the *teacher.* Teachers meet periodically with their peers in their own school to brainstorm suitable instructional adaptations for students. This has the advantage of being able to tap into ideas that other teachers have discovered in working with similar problems, and can have the side benefit of an increased comfort level when it becomes time to send a child on to his or her next teacher. Imagine being able to pass this child along to a teacher who has sat next to you for the past year in an assistance team meeting and helped you work out your instructional strategies for this child!

Having a strong, assistance-based team also provides a sense of community for teachers, a message of "We're all in this together," rather than "You're on your own." This sense of community can also be very reassuring to parents and their children.

20 Where can I go for help?

The days of teaching in isolation are over. No one person can handle the complex problems of today's learners without assistance. Luckily, there are many places to go for help and support:

- Connect with special education teachers and guidance personnel in your school; they have a wealth of information and resources to share.
- Consider team teaching, if possible. Often a competent teammate can provide solutions for problems that may elude you.
- Take advantage of schoolwide assistance teams to help you with problem solving. If none is available, talk to your administration about starting one.
- Connect with a knowledgeable teacher for peer coaching. If you are in a position to mentor someone else, do so.
- Read books and periodicals created for teachers.
- Take advantage of staff development resources; these are available through training organizations such as The Society for Developmental Education.*
- Do an ERIC search. ERIC has a wealth of information on specific educational topics, and is accessible via letter, phone, or the Internet:

  ERIC (Educational Resources Information Center)
  5207 University of Oregon
  Eugene OR 97403-5207
  1-800-LET-ERIC
  http://www.ed.gov/pubs/pubdb.html

* The Society For Developmental Education
Ten Sharon Road
PO Box 577
Peterborough, NH 03458
1-800-924-9621

Math Adaptations

General Adaptations

Space Cadets

organization

Help students learn to space their math problems on the page with this trick. Place a plastic six-pack can holder over a blank piece of paper. Teach the student to place one math problem inside each can ring. (The need to use this cueing system will soon disappear.)

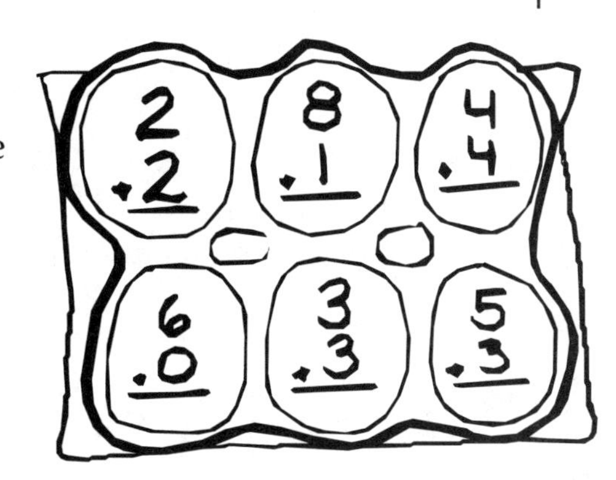

Math Map

sequencing

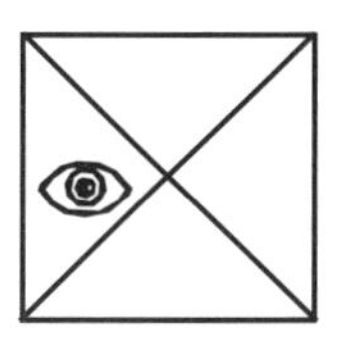

To assist some children with the necessary steps in doing math problems, provide them with a map which they can use as a visual organizer. Laminate the map and encourage the students to check off each step as they complete it.

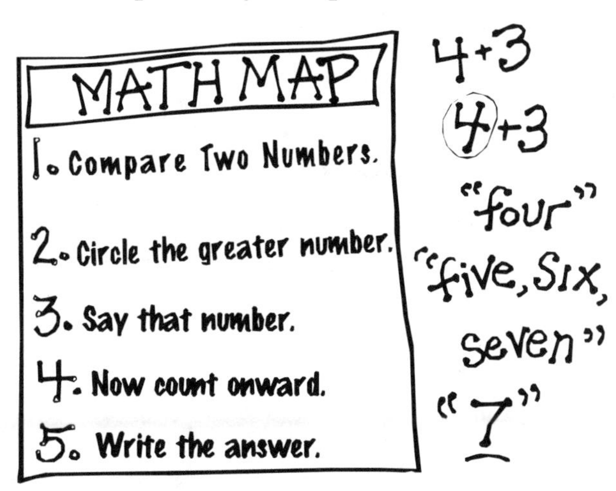

MORE General Adaptations

graphing

Personalized Graphing

Take a Polaroid photo of each student, or use a school photo. Laminate each child's picture and cover the back with Velcro or a magnet. Use the pictures for graphing exercises.

As an alternative, have students create their own business cards to use in graphing activities.

math

Group Work/Checking

Turn a math worksheet activity into a cooperative learning opportunity:

Divide the class into groups of four students. Laminate a set of math worksheets, and pass a laminated sheet to each group.

Ask one student to answer the first question, write his reply, and pass it on to another student. The group continues to do this until all the questions are answered. When the group has completed its entire sheet the students earn a bonus card, a ticket, or some other reward.

Math Manipulatives

A fun way to have math manipulatives is to make your own: cut colored overhead transparencies into a variety of geometric shapes and laminate them.

MORE Number Recognition

Just Monkeying Around

Purchase a "Barrel of Monkeys" set, and store it in the math center. Install a peg hook in the center and hang a number card on the hook. Students must assemble a monkey chain hanging off the hook to represent the number on the card. Change the number cards periodically.

This can also be used for addition: hang a card with a math fact on the hook and hang monkeys to match.

In a Row

ordinal numbers

consecutive numbers

Create a set of index cards with words representing the ordinal numbers "first" through "fifteenth" on them. (Use each word several times.) Deal three cards to each child, and have the children examine their cards and put them in order.

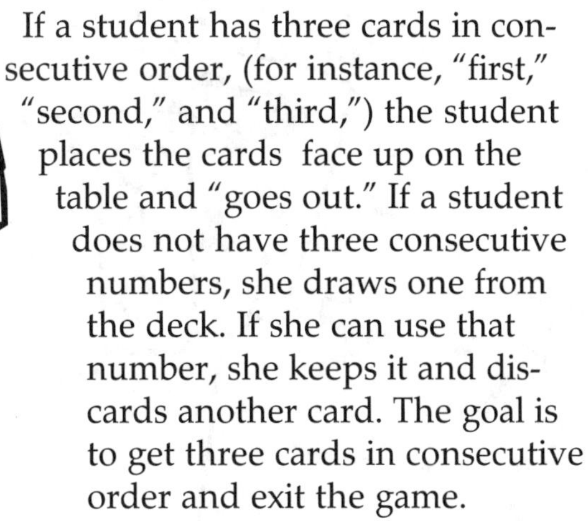

If a student has three cards in consecutive order, (for instance, "first," "second," and "third,") the student places the cards face up on the table and "goes out." If a student does not have three consecutive numbers, she draws one from the deck. If she can use that number, she keeps it and discards another card. The goal is to get three cards in consecutive order and exit the game.

This idea can also be used to review alphabetical order.

positive/
negative
numbers

Playing for Face Value

Use a deck of regular playing cards. Post the rules for the face value of each card:

Any card with a face	=	one
Aces	=	0
All red numbers	=	positive face value
All black numbers	=	negative face value

Deal five cards to each player. The players must examine their cards and decide whether they can create a number sentence with the cards they have; for instance:

Jack		**Queen**		**Ace**	**Five** *(Hearts)*	**Six** *(Spades)*		
(1	**+**	**1**	**+**	**0**	**+5)**	**-6**	**=**	**1**

The student with the highest score for each hand wins a "funny buck" (see page 72) which can be cashed in for treats at the end of the game.

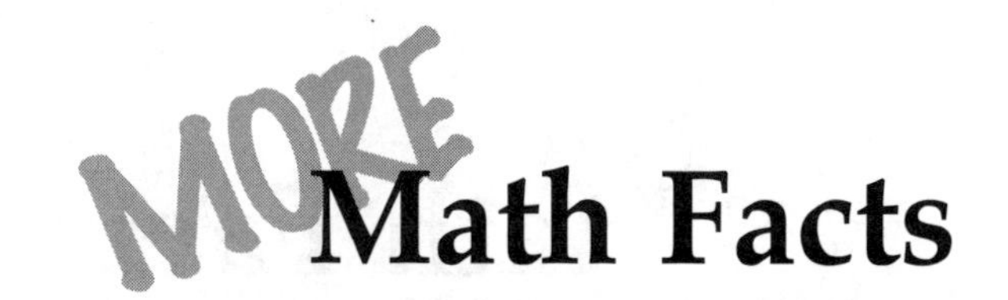

Math Facts

Dog-Gone Good Facts

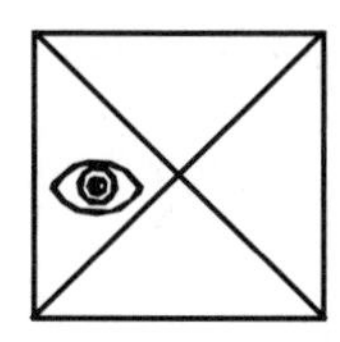

Use a cutout of a puppy. Write a math problem to be solved on the dog's body, leaving a blank space for the answer. Have the student write his answer in the appropriate space. Hide the answer under the dog's tongue or tail. Let the student check his own work.

Bean Hopscotch

gross motor skills

operational signs

Use dry white beans. Write a number from 1 through 9 on all sides of each bean. Draw a hopscotch board on the floor (or you may also draw it on a big piece of oak tag and tape it to the floor). In each square, write the last half of a math fact (for instance, +4, -2, etc.). Have students toss a bean onto a hopscotch square and perform the resulting operation. (The "9" bean lands on the "+4 square; 9+4=13.)

Spin the Bottle

operational signs

Write a number with its operational sign on a plastic half-gallon tea or juice bottle (for instance, +5). Distribute number buttons to the students. Have a child spin the bottle. When the bottle stops spinning and points to a particular child, that child will solve the math problem using the +5 and the number on her button. (For instance, a child wearing a button with "12" on it needs to answer "17.") If she is right, her classmates give her the thumbs-up sign, and she spins the bottle. If she's wrong, she can ask her classmates for help.

MORE Math Facts

fine motor skills

Plucking the Facts

Fill a large plastic container with cotton balls in two different colors. Give the student a pair of tweezers and a set of math fact cards suitable for his ability level. He must pluck the correct amount of cotton balls in each color to demonstrate each math fact.

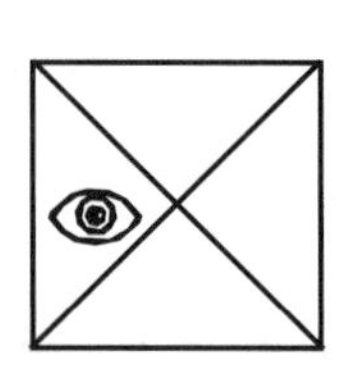

Flower Power

Cut out a 4" circle for the center of the flower. Write a number on it. Have students attach petals of math facts that result in the number in the center.

subtraction

operational signs

Hang Ups

Give a group of students a plastic clothes hanger and pinch clothespins. Have the students choose an amount of clothespins and hook them to the hanger. Ask a student to write the number of clothespins on the hanger on a piece of paper. Now have a student move a random number of clothespins to the right side of the hanger. Ask a student to write that number, and provide the operational sign. Now have the students write the number of clothespins remaining. (They need to provide the equal sign.) Ask the students how many other ways they can move the clothespins and use those three numbers in number sentences.

Math Facts

The Family Tree

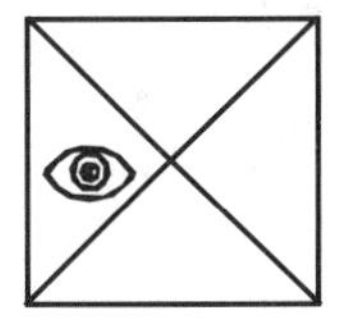

operational signs

Use a cutout of a tree for this activity. On the trunk of the tree, write three numbers to make a fact family. For example, write 3, 10, 7. Instruct the students to write a math fact on each branch of the tree to illustrate that fact family.

Factual Information

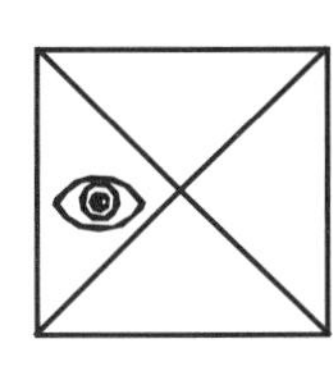

Write a number on the blackboard. Ask the children or teams of children to write down as many different ways as they can to describe the number. Have the teams share the facts and compare their math families.

Mailing Facts

sorting

Take a set of white envelopes and write a number from 1 to 20 on each. Designate one student as the mail carrier. Give the student a set of index cards with math facts that result in answers from 1 to 20. The mail carrier's task is to correctly deliver the index cards to the right envelope.

number recognition

fact recognition

Put Out the Fire

On a piece of oak tag, draw a picture of a house with smoke coming out of its roof. Laminate the picture. Now cut out and laminate a ladder for the rescue mission game.

Decide what concept you need to reinforce; for example, for some children, the objective might be number recognition. Write a different number to be identified on each rung of the ladder. The student has to "walk up the ladder" and identify each number. When she reaches the top rung, the fire is out, and she earns a fire hat sticker.

The objective for some children might be fact recognition. Write a number fact on each rung. Have the child climb each rung of the ladder, stating the correct answer to each problem.

eye-hand coordination

Swimming Mattress

Use an air mattress with indented air pockets. Place a number in each air pocket. Decide which math operation you will use for the toss, then toss two objects (coins, balls, beanie babies, etc.), so that they will land in two of the pockets. Whichever two numbers the objects land on, perform the chosen operation with the numbers.

This same activity can be used for place value or sight words.

Tied Up in the Facts

Decide which math facts you want to review. Punch holes down each side of a shoe box lid. On the left side of the lid, next to the holes, write numerals; on the right side write the math facts. Tie a large knot at one end of a piece of heavy twine. Have the students lace the twine through the holes on the left and right, matching the problems to the answers. Draw a pattern on the back of the lid for students to check themselves.

Coin Toss

eye-hand coordination

Use a shower curtain or Twister game sheet. Write ten math problems on the sheet; write their corresponding answers in different places on the same sheet. Toss a penny onto a math problem. You must toss another penny on the math problem's answer. Change the problems and answers depending on the level of the learner.

Butterfly Facts

Have each student trace around each of his feet. Write his name on each foot, and laminate the feet. Now draw an outline of a butterfly, and laminate the outline. On the center of the butterfly's body, write a number for review. Have students write math facts on each of their feet that result in the number on the butterfly's body. Have them place their math feet on each side of the butterfly's body for wings.

This could also be used for letter/ sound review: write or draw words with certain sounds on the wings, and write the letters to be reviewed on the butterfly's body.

Math Facts

Fruity Facts

Use large cutouts of any fruit containing seeds, but leave out the seeds. Students place the seeds on the fruit to illustrate fact families.

Math Fact Stampede

Provide the student with a 3" x 12" sentence strip or oak tag strip, plus a variety of stamps and stamp pads. The child chooses a math fact flash card from a set, and illustrates the problem using the sentence strip and stamps.

Inside/Outside Review

Stand the students on the floor in two circles, one inside the other. Make sure there are the same number of students in each circle; if you have an odd number of students, you or an aide can sit opposite the unpaired student.

Have each student face the child nearest her in the outer circle. The child in the inner circle gives the facing child a review problem to answer.

Now have the "outers" move two steps to the right; the "inners" give their new partners another review problem. This continues until all the children in the inner circle have worked with all the children in the outer circle.

This game is also fun to use when reviewing sight words, spelling words, states and capitals, and many other facts.

Math Facts

Domino Math

Review math facts with a set of dominoes. Each child selects a domino and uses the numbers represented by the dots on each side of the domino to create a number fact.

Here's how to create a large quantity of dominoes: place the original dominoes on the photocopying machine, copy them, then laminate the pages and cut apart the dominoes.

Fast Facts

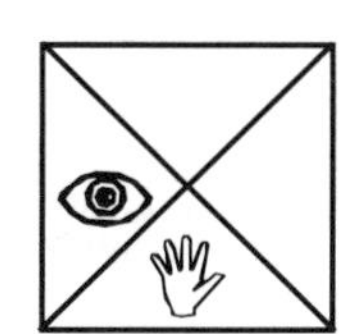

Write a "number of the day" on the blackboard each day. Throughout the day, whenever you have a moment to spare, call a child to the board to write a number sentence or fact family to represent the number.

Math Fact Search

Create a word search format, but use numbers instead of letters. The student's job is to find and circle three numbers that form a math fact family, vertically, horizontally or diagonally.

At first, create number searches using only one operation, such as addition. As the students' skill level increases, increase the number of different operations in the game. Have the students identify the operations they recognize as they circle fact families.

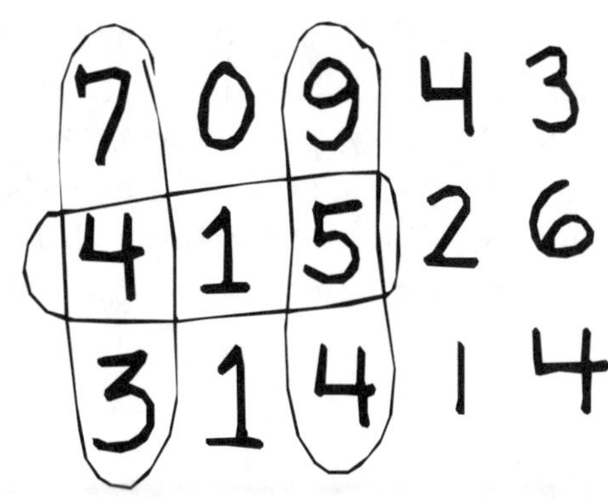

Bull's-Eye Math

Cut a circle out of a large piece of oak tag. Draw three concentric circles on the oak tag as a bull's-eye target, and color each section a different color. In each section of the circle write a variety of math problems, with the more difficult problems in the smaller, center circle.

Place the target on the floor. Assign a point value to each color of the target. Give the student a small beanie animal. The student chooses a problem in one section of the target, gives the correct answer, then tosses the beanie so that it lands in the correct section. If the student answers the problem correctly *and* hits the right circle with the beanie, she earns the assigned number of points.

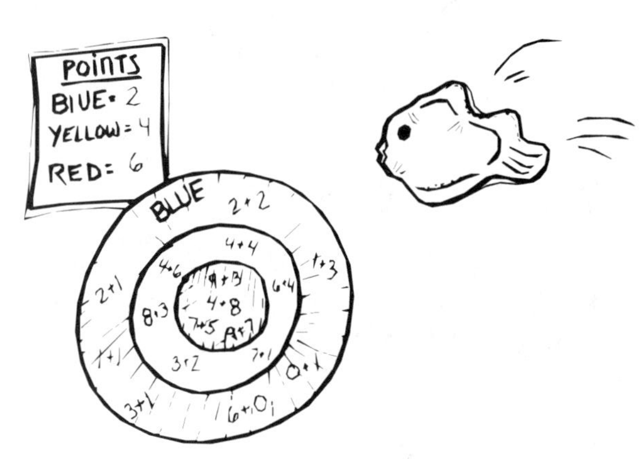

Another Bunch of Bull's-Eye Math

Draw a bull's-eye circle on the chalkboard, and color the sections with different colored chalk. Attach strips of Velcro to each section of the bull's-eye. The student tosses a Velcro ball (easily found at a toy store). The object is for the student to toss the ball into a section of the bull's-eye and perform the math operation that the teacher calls out. The more difficult problems are represented by the center circle.

Make sure you have math cards of three different levels of difficulty within the ability range of each student, so that if a struggling learner chooses the harder circle in the center of the bull's-eye, you have a math fact that he can answer.

Jumping Facts

Make a Jack-in-the box out of a large cardboard box. Cut a slit in the top of the box and put sentence strips with math facts on them inside the box. Write the answer to each math fact on the back of the sentence strips.

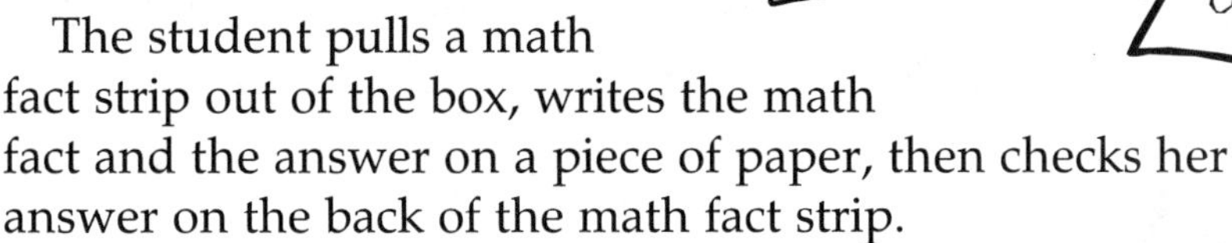

The student pulls a math fact strip out of the box, writes the math fact and the answer on a piece of paper, then checks her answer on the back of the math fact strip.

Stick to the Facts

Give each student a page or two of peel-off stickers, plus a blank 5" x 8" index card. Instruct the students to fold the cards in half, open them up, and apply a random number of stickers to the left and right sides of the card.

Have the students fold their cards in half with the stickers on the inside. On the front outside flap, have each student write a math problem based on the stickers inside: $4 + ? = 9$.

Laminate the cards and have the students pass them around for other students to solve.

MORE Math Facts

Fishy Facts

Cut out the head and tail of a fish body, and write the same number on each piece. Have students create fish scales from index cards and write math facts that result in the number written on the head and tail of the fish.

Iced Facts

Write a number on the inside of each section of a plastic ice cube tray. Cut out paper ice cubes, and write an addend or a multiplier on each cube: + 4, x 6, etc. Have the student shake out cubes from a bag or can into the ice cube tray, then perform the operation created by the combination of the paper ice cube and the number written inside the ice cube tray section. Have the students write the facts and solutions on a piece of paper.

Quick Draw

Use a set of number cards or numbered playing cards. Place the cards face down in a stack on the playing surface. Decide which operation will be used for the review, or have a child flip a coin for an operation. The first student draws the top two cards and performs that operation. The other players check for correctness. If the answer is correct, the student displays those two cards in front of him. If the answer is incorrect, the student places the cards on the bottom of the deck, and another student takes a turn.

= "12"

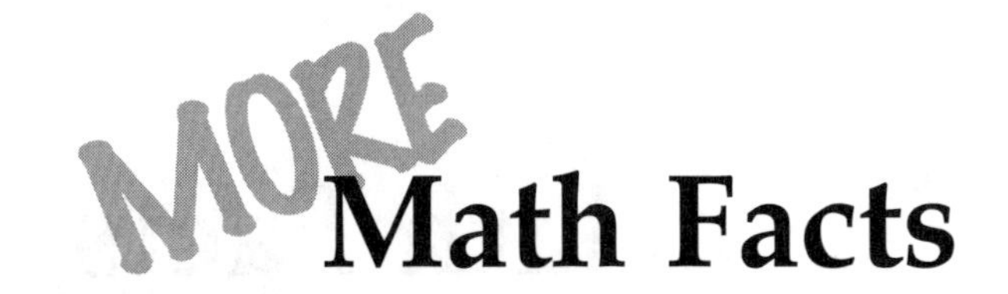

7-Up Facts

Turn the game of 7-Up into a fact review. Choose seven students to come to the front of the class. Give each of the seven students an index card with a math problem written on it. Have the rest of the students put their heads down on their desks.

Each of the seven students will tap a friend and hand the friend her card. When all seven students have given away their cards, the teacher says, "Heads Up, 7 Up." The students holding the index cards stand.

Next the teacher calls out an answer. The student who has the problem that matches that answer has a chance to guess who gave him the problem. If he guesses correctly, he switches places with his friend.

This game also can be used for spelling and vocabulary review.

Number, Number, What Can It Be?

Choose one student to be "it." Write a number on a piece of oak tag. Hold the card behind the student's back so the class can see it, and ask the class to feed the student hints about the number; for instance:

"It's bigger than 20, but less than 30."

"It's odd."

"It's divisible by 3."

MORE Math Facts

operational signs

Key Words

Cut large key shapes out of oak tag. Distribute two keys to each student. Have the student write a + on one and a – on the other.

Select one student to be the teaching assistant. Give the student a word problem to read: "There were four birds on a wire. Three flew away. How many are left? Show me the key sign." The students hold up the key that represents the operation they used to get the answer to the problem.

addition

Toss It Up

Write a single-digit number on a dot sticker in each cup of a muffin tin. Have the students flip two poker chips or tiddly winks into the tin. The students are to add the two numbers inside the cups in which the chips land. Have a calculator handy for self-checking. Subtraction and multiplication can be reviewed in the same fashion.

subtraction

Subtracting Clips

Have the students work in pairs to complete this subtraction review. Give each pair of students a box of large paper clips. The first student makes a chain out of a certain number of clips, for example, eight clips, and shows the "8 chain" to her partner. Next she tells her partner to close his eyes, removes some of the clips, and says to her partner, "I had eight clips. I hid two. Write the number sentence to show how many I have left on the chain." Have the children check each other's work. Continue the game, alternating checkers and writers.

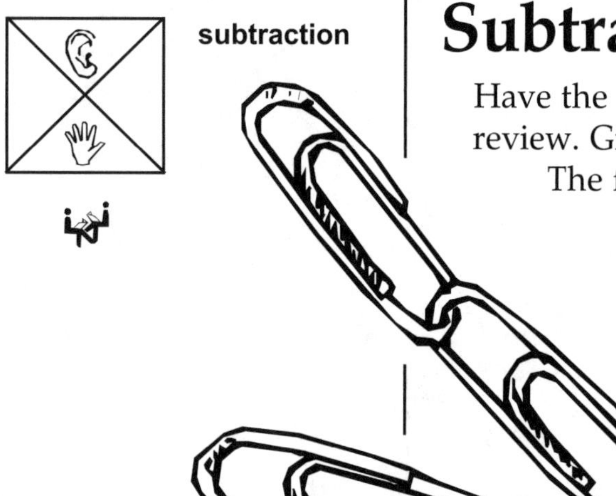

Floating Facts

subtraction

Purchase a supply of helium balloons. Select one child to come to the front of the room and give him a clown face or clown nose to wear if he chooses. Hand the child a certain number of balloons, then let him call on a friend to quiz him.

If Danny has five balloons in his hand and calls on Sara, she says, " Danny has five balloons. If the two red ones float away, how many will Danny have?" Danny releases the two red balloons and calls out the answer.

Guess If You Can

subtraction

Place cards with the numbers 1 to19 written on them in a shoe box or western hat. Designate one student to be "it." Have the student choose two cards from the hat. He must describe the two numbers by giving the result of a math fact.

For example, if the student chooses the numbers 15 and 9, he can cue the others by saying, "I have two numbers whose difference is 6." The child called upon to respond might ask, "Do you have 9 and 3?" The student in charge says, "No," writing the guess, 9-3, on the blackboard. The child who is "it" continues to call on students until someone guesses the right combination.

Math Facts

subtraction
addition
multiplication

Dice Review

Seat a small group of children around the blackboard. Write the number 100 on the board. Have the student to your left toss a set of dice and subtract the resulting number from 100. Have the class check the student's work. The person to the left of the first student then rolls the dice and subtracts that combination, the other students checking. This continues until the total of the equation reaches zero or as close to zero as possible.

Variations:

- Play this game with addition operations.
- Play this game in small groups; have each group keep track of their own results on a piece of paper.
- Have each group of students write the number 2 on a piece of paper. The first student in the group rolls one die. The members multiply the number by 2. Continue playing until one group reaches 100.

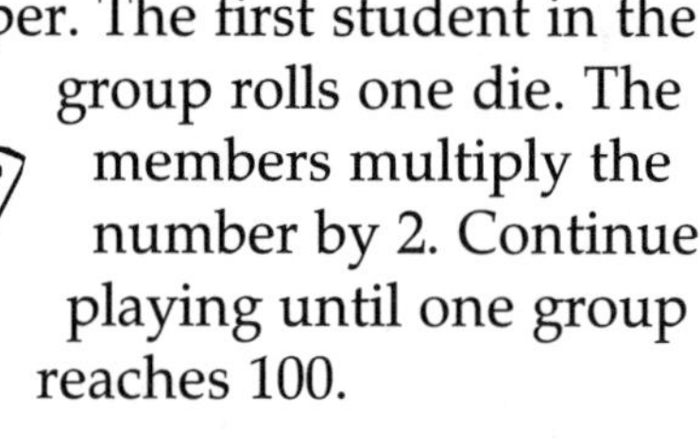

multiplication
addition

With a Roll of the Dice

Use a pair of game dice. Have the students roll the dice, multiply the two numbers, and write their answers on a sheet of paper. Each answer needs to be added to the previous one. The first student to reach 50 is the winner.

My Own Multiplication

sets

multiplication

Give the students a handful of rubber bands. Have them decide what multiplication facts they will review. Glue the rubber bands on paper to create circles for number sets.

For fun homework or class work, have the students glue objects inside the rubber bands to represent multiplication facts.

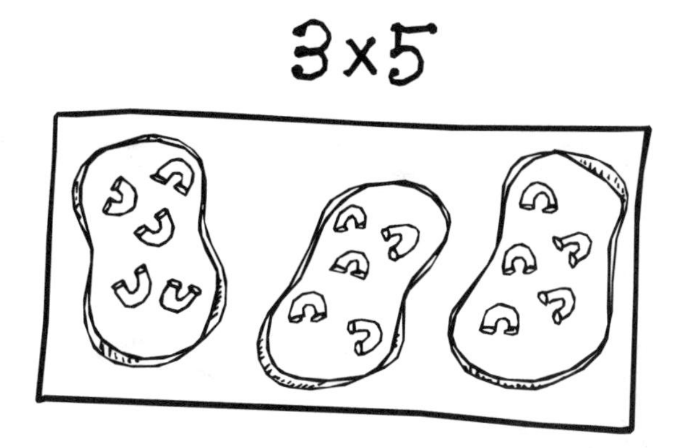

The Ease of the Steps

division

sequencing

Divide the students into teams of four to review the steps of long division:

1. Divide
2. Multiply
3. Subtract
4. Bring Down

Assign a color to each step of the division problem. For example:

Divide = yellow; multiply = purple; subtract = black; bring down = orange. Pass a set of markers in these colors to each group of students, one marker per student. Tell the students that whatever color their marker is, they need to perform that step of the division problem.

Give each group of students a division problem; the students need to pass the problem among themselves to arrive at the solution.

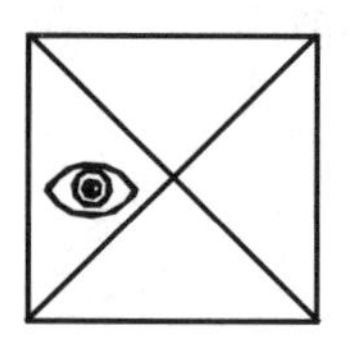

Gator Than

This visualization helps children understand the concept and remember the symbols for "greater than" and "lesser than."

Write two numbers on the blackboard, leaving plenty of space between the numbers. Draw a gaping gator mouth between the two numbers which points to the larger number. Tell the children that the hungry gator always eats the bigger number.

MORE Number Lines

Counting On

addition

When first teaching the concept of addition, teach the students how to "count on" using a number line:

1. Touch the greatest number.
2. Say that number.
3. Count on from that number, until you count as many steps as the smaller number.

Hopping Number Lines

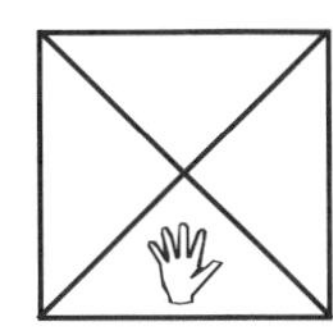

Teach students to use a plastic bunny to hop forward (+) and backward (-) on number lines to reinforce the concept of math operations.

Number Line Guess

Distribute a number line to each child. Assign one student the task of being "it."

Give the student a number. Ask the student to describe to the class where that number falls on the number line without saying what the number is. For example, " I have a number that is greater than 4," "This number is six hops to the right of 3," or "The number is two hops to the left of 11. "What is the number?" Students take turns describing numbers using the number line.

MORE Place Value

Place Value Puzzles

Create puzzles out of oak tag or construction paper, using seasonal shapes (snowmen, leaves, turkeys, etc.). Cut each shape in half, write a number on one half, and describe the number by place values on the other half as shown. Students match the pieces and read the answers.

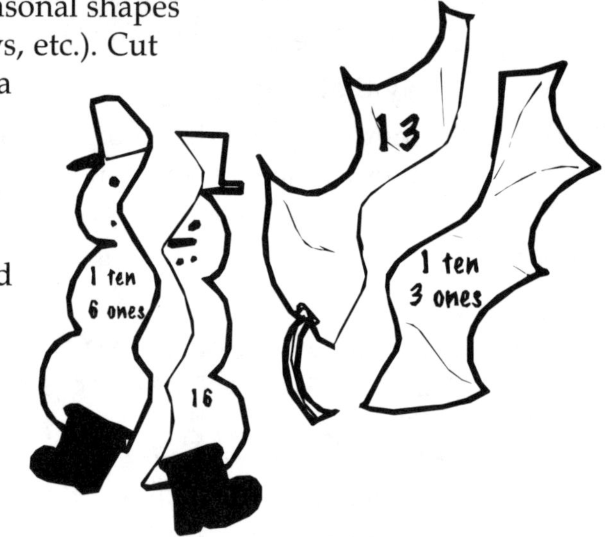

Bean Stalks

Students can help assemble this game before they use it:

1. Glue 10 dried beans (or use rigatoni) to a popsicle stick. Each child makes at least ten of these popsicle sticks with ten beans on each.
2. Place the sticks in an empty coffee can or juice can.
3. Place a cup of loose beans in each work area.

When reviewing place value, write a number on the board, such as 46. Have each student use the sticks (4) and the loose beans (6) to demonstrate tens and ones.

Fraction Cakes

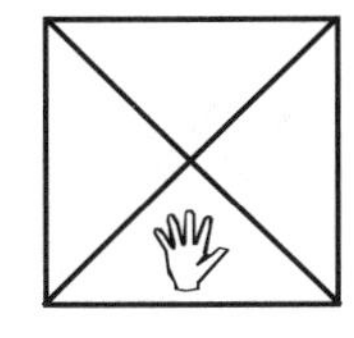

Give each student an 8" x 10" piece of brown paper to make a chocolate cake. Practice dividing the cake into eighths. Decorate 2/8 of the cake with "sprinkles" (glitter); use stars on 1/8 of the cake, etc.

Fraction Faction

Using the same framework as "Simon Says," have fun, reviewing fractions: "Simon Says, 'Show me 3/10's of your fingers,' " or "Show me 1/4 of the boys in this classroom."

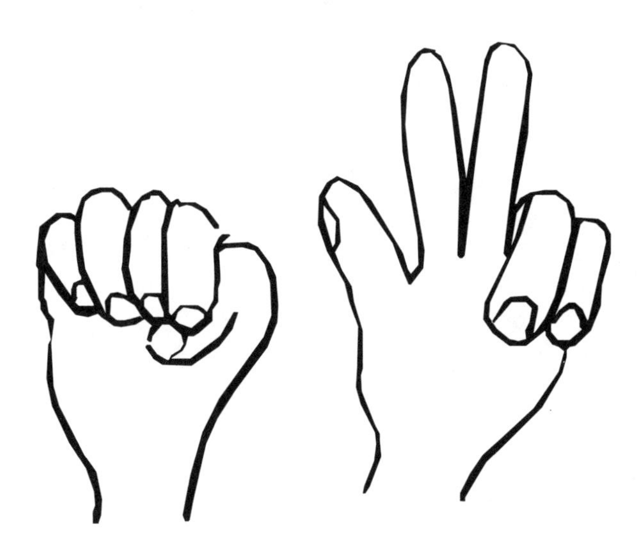

MORE One-to-One Correspondence

counting

Math Centers

To reinforce the concept of one-to-one correspondence, create a chart for the math center with places for the number of clothespins representing the number of students who can work at the center at one time. Students take a clothespin from a bucket and put it on the chart as they go to work in the center. If the chart is full, they must find another center.

For students who are unable to make choices, put their names on the clothespins and assign them a center.

Shaping Up the Facts

addition

subtraction

Try this idea at a learning center. Have a variety of colored shapes cut out of paper. Give the students a math sheet with directions such as:

"To make your design, you will need:

1 + 2 green triangles

5 - 2 orange circles

9 - 8 pink squares

Assemble your shapes and see what kind of picture you can make."

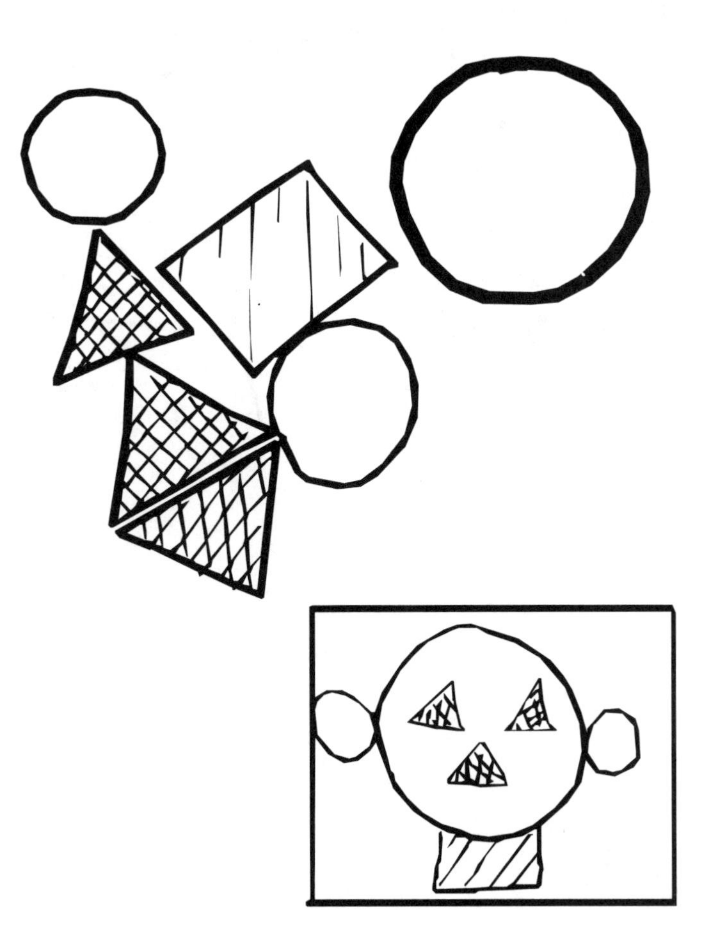

MORE Sorting and Classifying

Running Wild

Let your imagination run wild when helping your students grasp the concept of sorting and classifying. The students can sort m&m's and candy hearts by color, or potato chips and crackers by type. You can also get really creative and have your students sort sterilized and bleached chicken and beef bones.

Money

Coupon Clippers

counting

When working on a money unit, have the students cut coupons from old magazines or newspapers, and match actual coins to the money value on the coupon.

Get in Order

addition

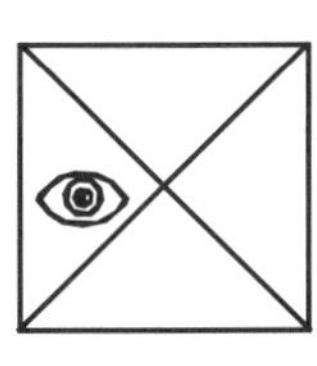

Give your students leftover order forms from class book clubs, magazine clearinghouse companies, catalogs, etc. Give each of them a "Gift Certificate" for a designated amount of money. They must order the items they want without exceeding their gift certificate amount.

Dining Out

addition
counting

Ask each student to bring a restaurant menu to school, then give out individual Ziploc bags of money. Each student fills out an order form listing all the food items he can buy from his menu with the amount of money in his Ziploc bag.

MORE Money

multiplication

Changing Coupons

Clip store coupons onto index cards, and write a monetary value for the featured product on the card below the coupon. Have students figure out what they would pay for the item if the coupon amount was worth double its face value.

addition

Throwing Money Away

Place a picture of a garbage can on the floor. Tape a piece of masking tape on the floor three feet away from the picture. Have the children line up in two teams behind the tape.

Give each team money value cards (all under a dollar) to toss at the can. The object is for the students to toss the cards onto the can, and be the first team to throw a dollar away without going over that amount.

counting

Face Value

Some children may need a number chart on their desks to add like and unlike coins; for example, to add a dime and a quarter. Have the student start on the 10-cent square on the chart, mark the square with a place mark, and count 25 places to the 35-cent square.

Slapping the Bucks

greater than/ less than

Teach students how to play "Slap Jack." Now play for money. Using the money cards from the "Go Fish" game, divide the cards equally between two players. As the students flip cards in their pile over one at a time, they see who can slap the card with the higher money value first. If correct, the slapper gets to keep the card. The winner is the player with the most cards at the end.

Fishing for Money

addition

Use a set of money flash cards for this game. (These cards can be found in school supply catalogs or you can make your own.)

Teach students the concept of playing "Go Fish." Distribute ten flash cards to each player. The students' goal is to collect enough cards to total exactly $1.00.

The students ask for money values; for instance, a student holding a quarter card and a half-dollar card may ask, "Give me all your quarter cards or all your cards totaling a quarter." If the other player doesn't have any of those cards, he says, "Go Fish," and the first student draws from the pile until he get the cards he needs. As students collect cards which total $1.00, they discard those cards. The first person to get rid of all his cards wins.

Spending the Dough

addition

Choose two students to be your personal shoppers. Give these partners a set amount of money. Send them to the cafeteria, school store, or classroom snack bar. Instruct the students about how much money they have and what your requirements are: "I gave you $1.10. Please go to the cafeteria and buy me something for lunch that costs no more than that and where you'll get 20 cents in change."

MORE Telling Time

Time and Temperature

Select one student to be the weather forecaster and let him pick a partner of his choice. Give the forecaster a toy microphone and radio set-up, and a piece of paper with the time and temperature written on it. As the forecaster announces the time, his partner sets a clock and toy thermometer correctly.

time

sequencing

My Personalized Daily Clock

Have the students cut out four clock faces; or give them four paper plates to use.

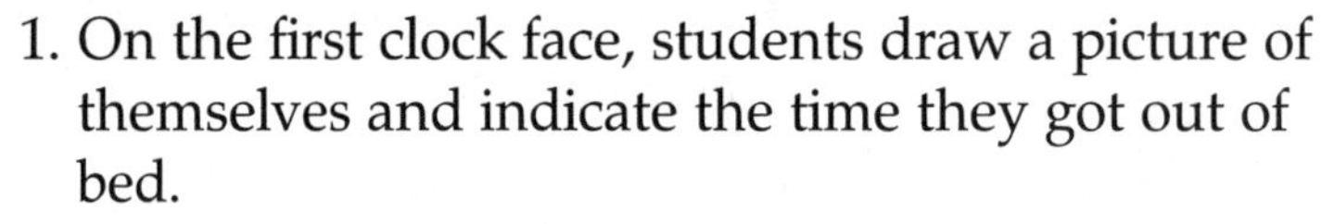

1. On the first clock face, students draw a picture of themselves and indicate the time they got out of bed.
2. On the next clock face, students draw hands to indicate the time of the first event of their day, then illustrate that event.
3. On the third clock face, they indicate the time of their second activity of the day, and illustrate it.
4. On the fourth clock face, they indicate the time of the last event of the day, and illustrate it.

This activity can be expanded to cover the times of all events of the day.

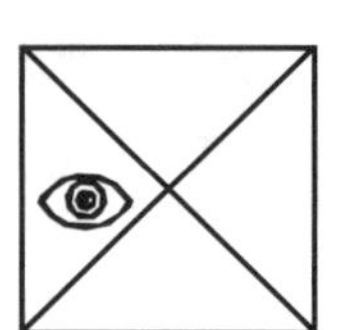

Color-Coded Hands

Color-code the clock hands throughout the school the same colors: yellow for the minute hand, blue for the hour hand. This helps students who are having trouble differentiating between the minute and hour hands to do so.

Rock Around the Clock

Use this activity at a center or as a whole group activity. Provide each child with a clock face with the numerals and hands. Use a spinner chart with minutes, in fives, on the chart. One student spins the spinner. Whatever number he lands on, the rest of the students must correctly cover the corresponding clock number. If the student lands on 10, the class must cover the 2 on the clock; if the student lands on 45, the class must cover the 9. (You can use Bingo chips to cover the numbers.) The first student who covers all of his clock numbers gets to choose whether to be first or last in line for the day.

First and Last Hands

When teaching students how to discriminate between the hour hand and the minute hand, have each student write his first name on a color-coded hour hand. Have him write his last name on the minute hand. Attach the hands to a paper plate clock. Remind the student that he will always say his first name (hour) first and last name (minutes) last.

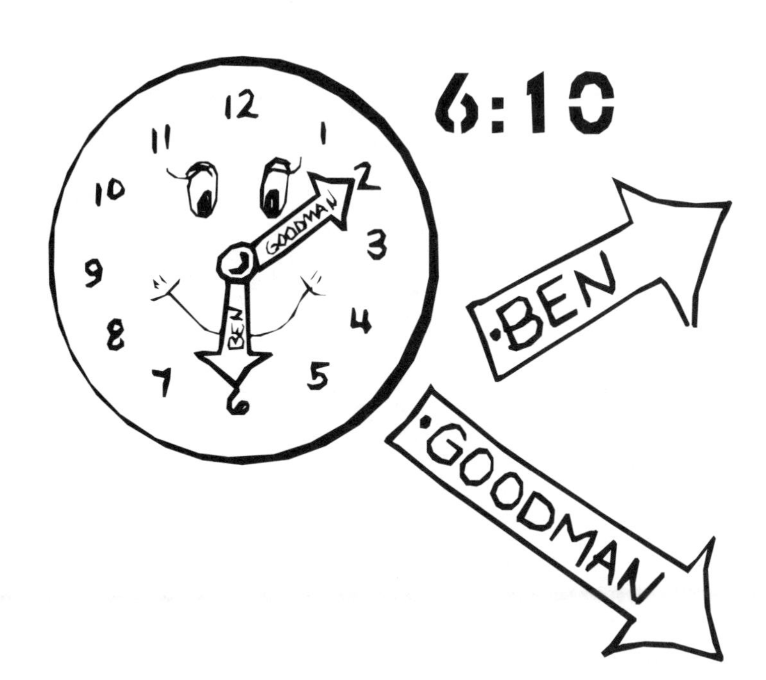

Making It Up

Use a nonstandard form of measurement to help the children understand the concept of measuring:

- Give them paper clips to measure how big their hand is.
- In March, use a shamrock to measure how many shamrocks tall they are.
- Use a footprint cut out to see how many feet wide they are.
- Use red Swedish fish to measure the desks.

Reading Adaptations

Motivation

A Recipe for Reading

book reports

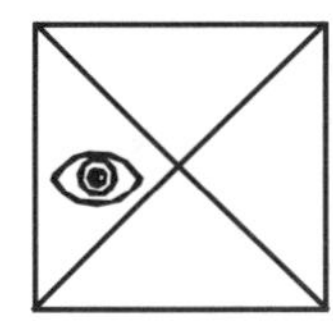

To help students motivate themselves, give them each an empty recipe file box and a batch of index cards. Ask the students to guesstimate how many books they can read by a given date, and write each student's guess on the top or front of his file box. Every time the student reads a book, he fills out a card with the book's title, author, characters, and setting, plus the student's favorite part of the book, and places it in the file box. This practice inspires students to work toward reaching and beating their goals in the designated time frame.

King / Queen for the Day

book completion

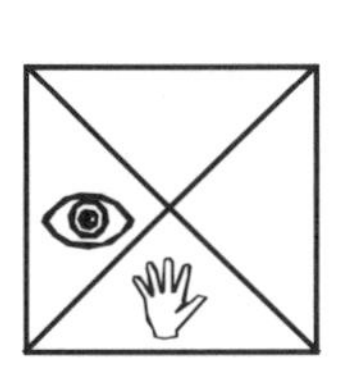

Have each student create a crown or headband; when she finishes reading or listening to an assigned story, she gets to put a gold star or fancy sticker on her crown. The children will wear their jeweled crowns proudly.

book reports

Banana Split Party

Pick a date as class "banana split day." Assign reading tasks and match them to a specific banana split ingredient:

Banana:	Read a book about a dog.
Vanilla ice cream:	Read a book about a planet.
Chocolate ice cream:	Read a book about a turtle.
Strawberry ice cream:	Read a book about a family.
Chocolate syrup:	Write a book review.
Whipped cream:	Read a story to another classroom.
Nuts:	Write about a story problem and how it was solved.
Cherry:	Read a story to the principal.

Make sure you adjust the assignments for a variety of ability levels.

Each student picks the ingredient she wants to supply and completes the necessary reading assignment. On the day of the party, each student brings in her assigned banana split ingredient.

This is a good cooperative learning opportunity; children can negotiate with each other as they plan to do the assignments necessary for all the ingredients.*

Make sure you let parents know about this party ahead of time!

* Make sure you know of any food allergies among your students, and avoid exposing those children to foods that could cause an allergic reaction.

Go Fish

higher-level thinking
comprehension

Write problem-solving questions on a school of cut-out fish and keep them handy in a fish bowl on the teacher's desk. The questions can be based on thematic units they have studied.

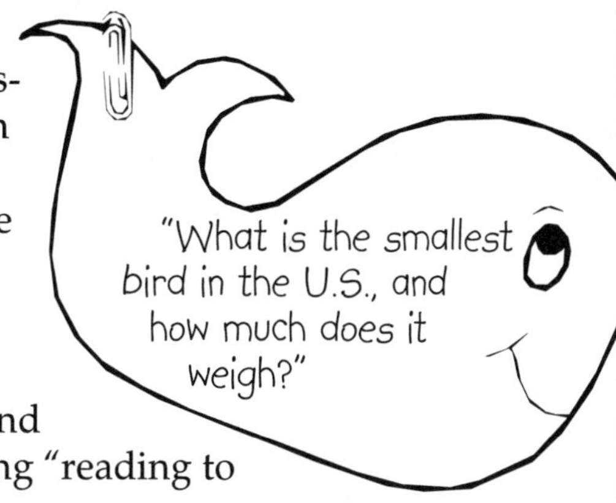

When children need a filler activity, they can catch a fish and answer the question by applying "reading to learn" strategies.

"I Can Read"

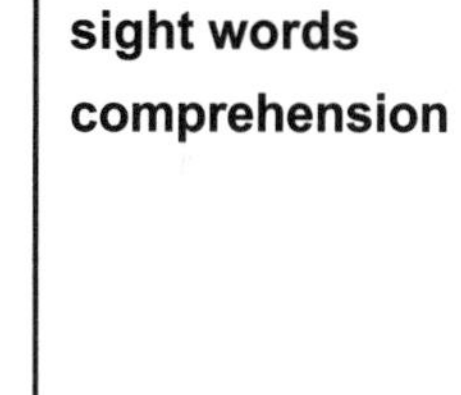

sight words
comprehension

Students can use pictures and words cut out of magazines and newspapers to create an "I Can Read" book. Have each student choose eight or ten words she can read. Paste each word and a matching picture on a separate piece of paper. Bind the pages together into a book.

The pages will look like this:

TIDE
I can read TIDE
Now...
I can read Ride.
I can read Wide.
I can read Side.

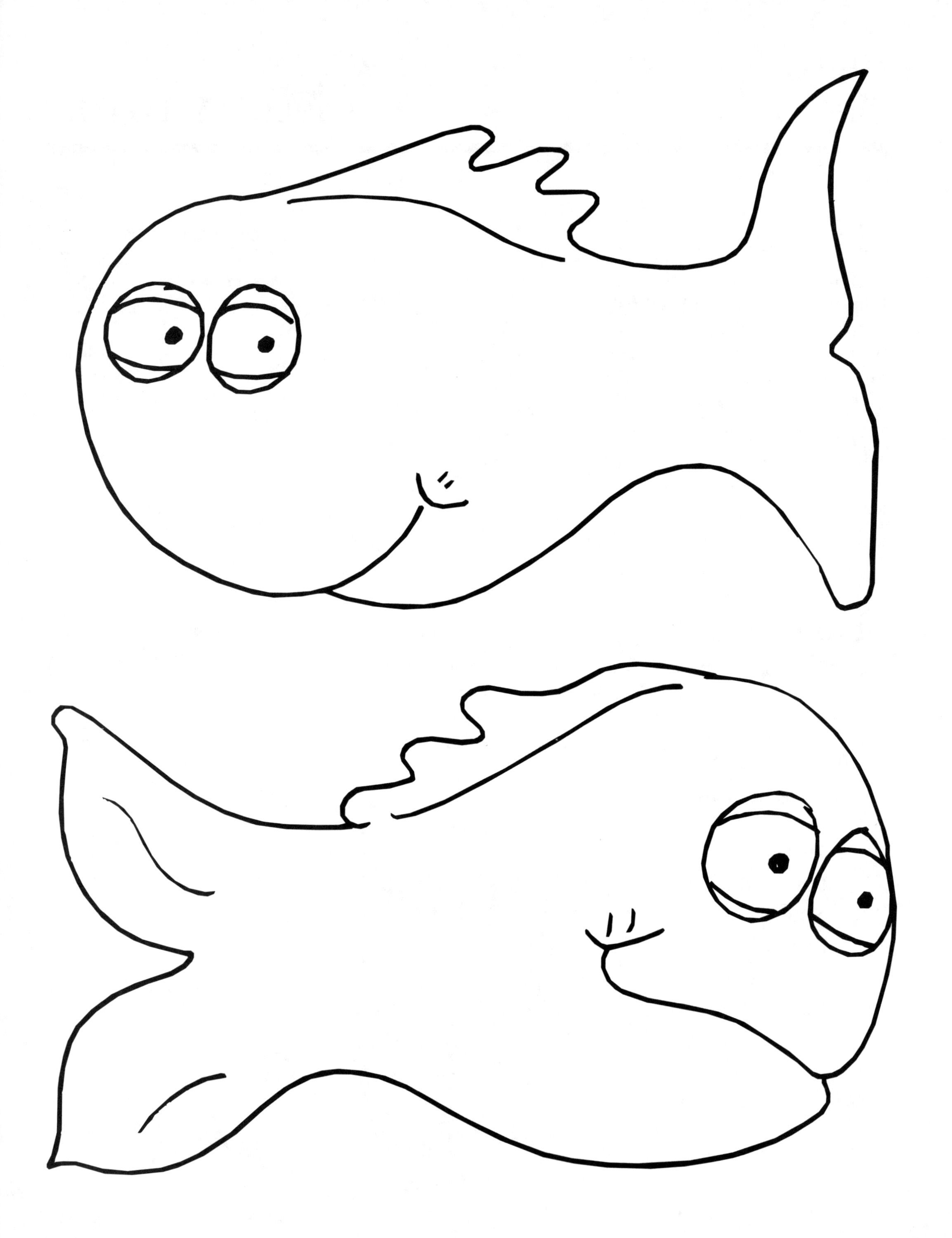

"More I Can Read"

Use this activity to remind students of everything they have learned to read; this is a good way for a reluctant reader to measure progress.

Bind pages together into a book that demonstrates all the different ways a student can read; entitle the book, "More I Can Read." The first page can have color swatches, but no words, showing that the child can read colors. The next page can contain shapes. The third page can show a child going up and down the steps with the words "up" and "down" on the page to show the child understands direction words. Include pictures to read, as well as "feeling faces," weather codes, the ABC's, numbers, and names of classmates.

sight words
environmental print
comprehension

Motivation

sight words
environmental print
following directions

Scavenger Hunt

Engage both students and parents in this back-to-school-night activity. Give each family group a clipboard, a marker and a set of written instructions to read and follow. For instance, the directions might read:

> "Take your family to the room where you go to do research. Have the parent with you place his or her initials on line seven. Next, go to the room where running is allowed. Have the teacher in that room sign line six."

Make each set of directions different, and make sure the parents get to visit parts of the building important to the student. Have all the family groups meet in the classroom at the end of the scavenger hunt for refreshments.

Auction Leftovers

Create and distribute "book bucks" that children can earn for appropriate behavior in the classroom (see page 72). At the end of each marking period, encourage students and parents to donate books the children have successfully read and enjoyed. Set a date and have an auction so the children can buy the donated books with their book bucks.

one-to-one correspondence

Recycling

When a child has finished reading a book at home, encourage parents to donate the book (with the child's permission) to the classroom. Each time a child donates a book, the teacher writes the child's name on a ticket and puts it into a ticket box. On the last Friday of each month, the teacher places all the recycled books on a table, and pulls each ticket, one by one, from the ticket box. As a child's name is read, she chooses a new book from the table; if Janie has donated ten books to the class during the month, she gets ten new books on Recycling Day.

Remember, there will always be some children who will pick their own donated books to take back home again, especially if it is one of their favorites.

Scavenger Hunt

	PEOPLE TO SIGN
1. Show your family where your seat of choice is. Do you dare to show inside your desk?	____________ Family member's initials
2. Share a published story or a journal writing.	____________ Your initials
3. Walk your family to the place in the school where we can do research or look for our favorite authors.	____________ Librarian's initials
4. Skip with your family to the Music Room. Have ____________ (teacher's name) sign your sheet.	____________ Music teacher's initials
5. From this area, see if you can give your family directions to the room where you do exercises and an obstacle course.	____________ PE teacher's initials
6. Hunt very hard to see if you can find the leader of the building.	____________ Principal's initials
7. Hungry? Stroll down to the room your tummy likes best. Bring your teacher 1 cookie.	____________ Family member's initials
8. Can you find the Art teacher? Have him sign with a red crayon.	____________ Art teacher's initials
9. If you are in the mood to show off your computer skills, see if you can connect your family to the Internet or a favorite computer activity.	____________ Your initials
10. Finally, return this paper back to your teacher, put your clipboard away and have a safe trip home!	____________ Teacher's initials

5
BOOK BUCK
Book Bucks

5
Funny Bucks

1
BOOK BUCK
Book Bucks

1
Funny Bucks

5
BOOK BUCK
Book Bucks

5
Funny Bucks

1
BOOK BUCK
Book Bucks

1
Funny Bucks

5
BOOK BUCK
Book Bucks

5
Funny Bucks

Parent Postcards

sight words

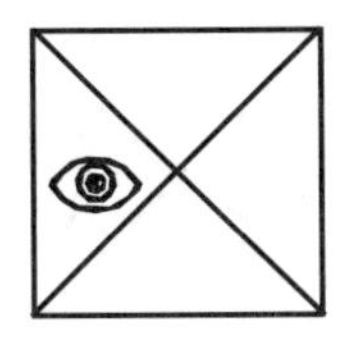

Send blank postcards home to parents, or distribute them at back-to-school night. Ask parents to write an encouraging note to their child and put it in their child's lunch at least once a week. Provide the parents with a sample set of encouraging notes. You can also send weekly vocabulary words home to parents and ask them to incorporate some of the words into the notes.

Tab It Words

sight words
rhyming/
decoding/
phonics

Here is a fun way to review sight words, letter blends or rhyming words. Create a poster with a pull tab in various shapes. If the students are reviewing word clusters beginning with the letter blend "fl," create a flower with the letters "fl" written on it, and next to the "fl" a pull tab with word endings on them, such as -ower, -orist, -y, etc. For "st" words, design a stop sign with a pull tab.

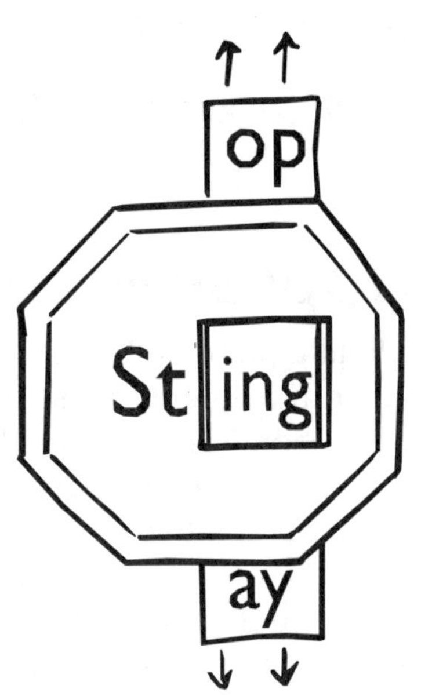

Sight Word Tie-Ups

sight words
decoding

Place a picture representing the sight word you want to review in the center of an index card. In each of the corners of the card write a word; one of the words correctly identifies the picture on the card. Have the student string yarn from the picture to the correct word. On the back of the card, draw a line showing the positions of the picture and the correct word, so that students may check their own work.

This activity can be adapted for math facts or spelling words.

MORE Motivation

sight words
phonics
decoding

Steps to Decoding

Often children who have difficulty decoding words in context need visual cues for the steps involved. Design a staircase format to use in the room as a reference chart:

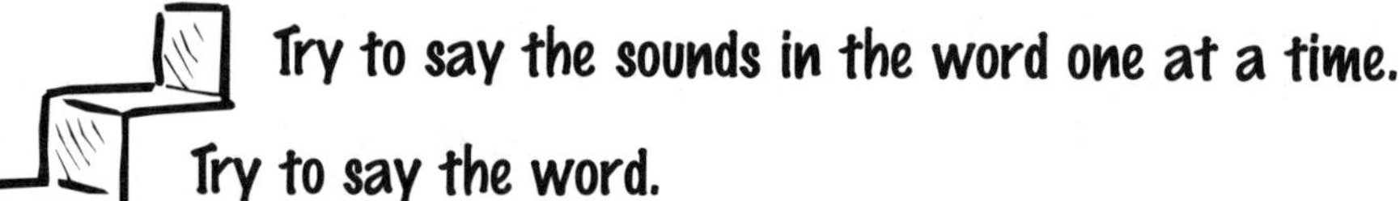

Look for letter sounds you might know.

Look for known words inside the word.

decoding
sight words
antonyms

Opposites Attract

Fold a piece of 9" x 12" construction paper in half lengthwise. Divide the top section into four sections, and cut to create four equal flaps. On the outside of the flap draw a picture of the first word; on the inside, write that word. Lift the flap and draw a picture of the opposite, or write the opposite word, under the flap. Have one student state the opposite of the word on top to his partner; his partner lifts the flap and checks.

group
motivation
book reports

Rewarding Puzzles

Create a large puzzle by cutting a bulletin-board sized picture into pieces. Set a class goal for monthly reading: a total of forty pages a day, for instance, for the whole class. Each time the class reaches its goal, a piece of the puzzle is pinned up on the bulletin board. When the students complete the puzzle, the whole class wins a prize.

Reading Before Bed

Hold a school or class sleep-over. Encourage the students to bring their favorite books and their sleeping bags to school, and read to each other before going to bed. If you can't actually sleep over, have a mock pajama party during the day.

Context Detectives

decoding
phonics
dictionary skills
context

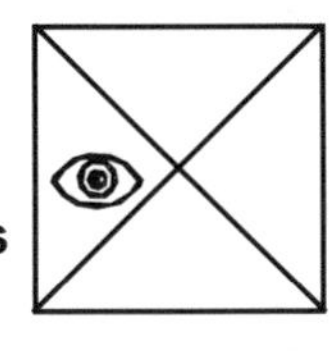

Find ten to fifteen words in the dictionary that the students do not know. Write each of the words and its definition on an index card.

Have the children work in groups. The first team member studies the word and its definition and then writes one or two sentences using that word in context. That context clue is passed to the next member. If that member is able to define the word by using context clues only, the team receives a point.

Reader of the Week

book reviews

Appoint a reader of the week. Allow the child a prized place to sit — a rocker, a gold throne, or a claw-foot tub — and read to the class.

Take a Polaroid picture of the event. Paste the picture on the front of a manila folder, and pass the folder around the room so that each child can write inside the folder and describe what he or she liked about the story that was just read.

Display the folder in the classroom for a while, then send it home with the reader of the week.

school helpers
awareness
reading aloud

Book Signing Party

After a child publishes a story in the classroom, set up a time for the author to autograph the story and share it with others. The student can go on a publicity tour to the nurse, the cafeteria, the custodian, and the principal to share the happy event.

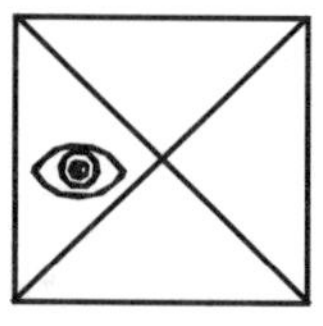

communication
comprehension

Reading by the Board

How many of us enjoy reading the message boards at the national conferences we attend? Children will enjoy this too. Designate a large bulletin board in the school or in your wing of the school where children write and read messages from peers.

poetry
reading aloud
comprehension

Poetic Justice

Each month, choose four poems and type them on squared-off index cards. Laminate the poems, and attach one poem to each side of a cardboard cube box. Have the children sit in a circle, and invite one student to roll the cube. The student reads or recites, alone or with a partner, whichever poem lands on top when the cube is rolled.

If you send the poems home with students so they can rehearse them in advance, most students will feel comfortable reciting them in class.

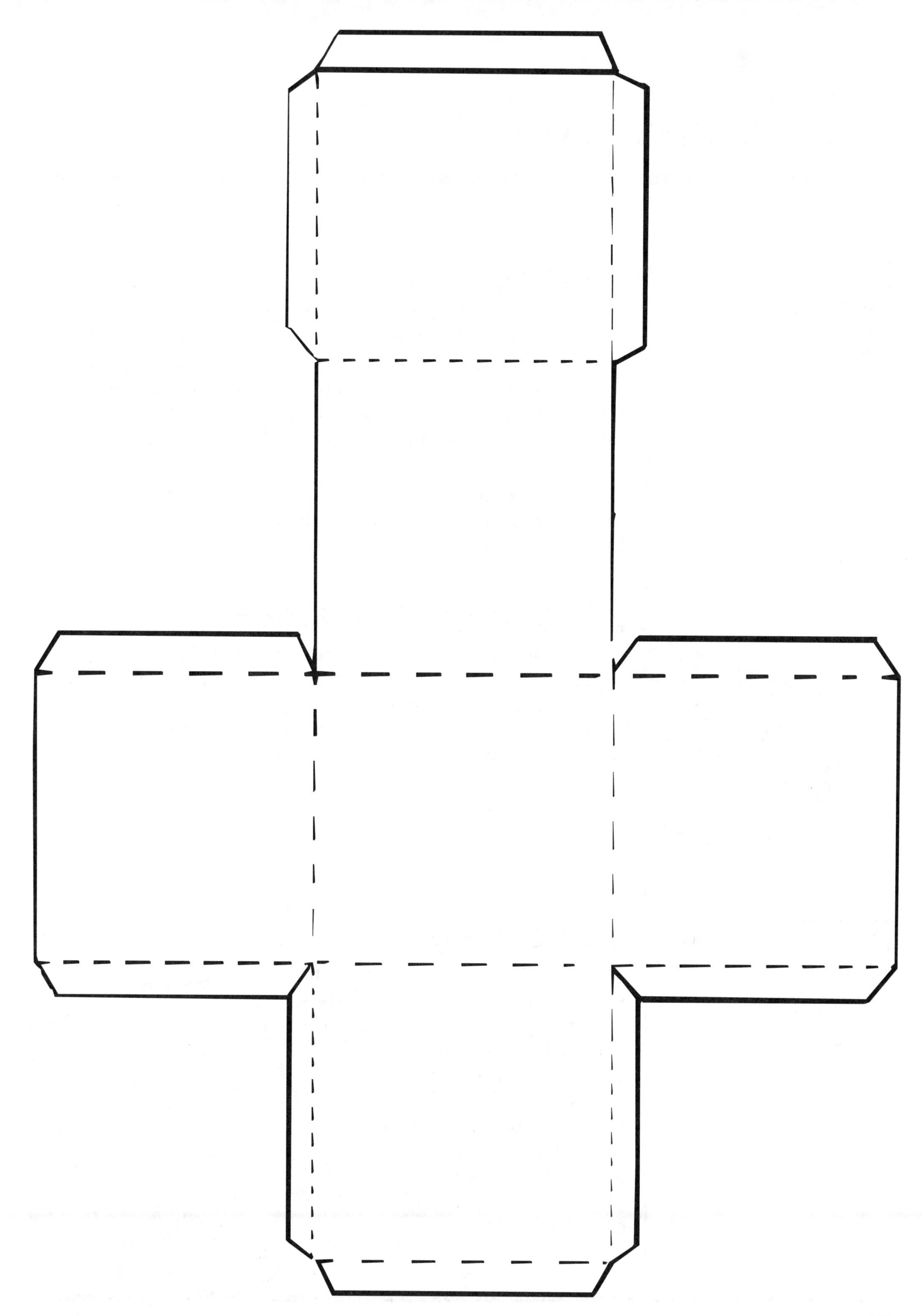

MORE

Management

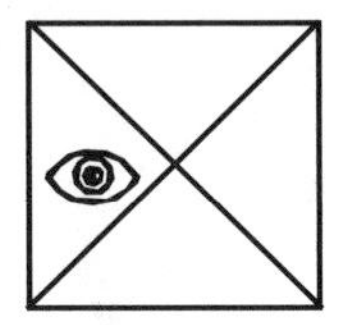

Taking Turns

Use folders of different colors to keep track of whose turn it is to read in class. Inside each folder, write the names of four students. Choose one folder at the beginning of the day; the children whose names are in that folder will know that they will get an opportunity to read aloud that day. Choose a different color folder each day, to make sure you're giving each group of children a fair chance to read.

If you have "more kids than colors," make a large design on one folder of each color, to distinguish the two yellow folders from each other, for instance.

Flipping for Names

Attach an index card for each child to a clipboard. This provides a handy place to record that you've worked individually or conferenced with a particular child. Get support personnel in the classroom in the habit of recording their interactions with each child, as well.

comprehension

Fun Sheets

Ever wonder what to do with leftover skills worksheets? Fill in the answers, then cut them apart, so that the questions and answers are separated. Laminate them and attach a small magnet to the back of each piece. Use a jelly roll pan or a cookie sheet for the back board. Have the students manipulate the sheets to reassemble the correct answers.

Status Symbols

Attach a small school photo of each of your students to individual 5" x 8" index cards. On the backs of the cards, list the children's full name, address, phone number, and birthdate. Children can use these personal flash cards at centers to review vital statistics, to learn to copy the information, to play Class Clue, or to practice writing their names.

self-awareness
comprehension
writing

Addressing Favorites

As soon as a child in your classroom knows his entire address, write it on a school or local postcard and mail it. The child will quickly recognize the benefits of reading and receiving mail.

motivation
self-awareness
parental involvement

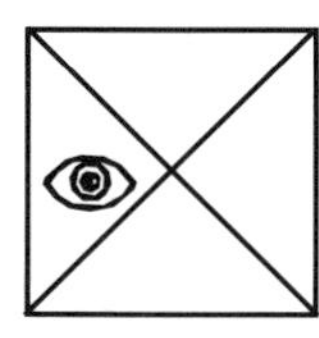

I Just Called to Say

On the day a child in your classroom first recites her entire phone number, call her at home in the evening to offer your congratulations.

motivation

comprehension
retelling
parental involvement

Story Clouds

Use this activity to help students recall and retell the story of the day. Give parents the activity's goals and the steps necessary for its completion ahead of time.

After reading a class story, give each child a cloud cutout with a story illustration on it. The child's responsibility is to take the story cloud home and tell the story to his parents. The parents write the story onto the cloud as the child dictates it; the child colors the illustration and returns the cloud to school.

Freeze the Scene

comprehension
book reviews
role play

After completing an assigned book, invite the students to work in pairs or small groups and recall the most memorable scene from the book. Ask each group to "freeze the scene" and stand silently in front of the group. The rest of the class has to guess which scene or chapter is being depicted.

Condensed Version

retelling

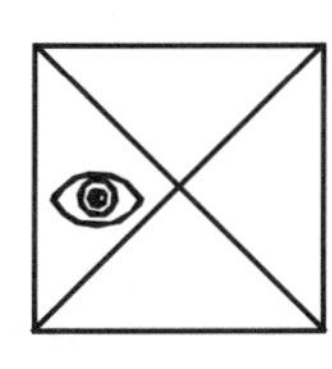

Pair students by reading level and give them a paragraph from a newspaper or magazine written at their level. Have them read the paragraph and condense it to five sentences, including all the important facts in their condensed version.

Listen Up

comprehension

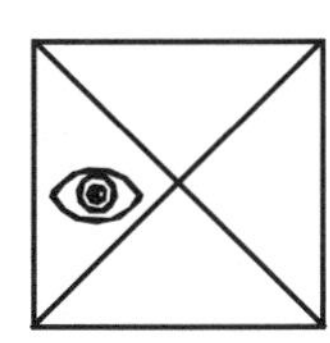

Read a story to the class. Use visual webbing to help the students listen for specific information; for example: main character, other characters, sequence of events, places, and objects.

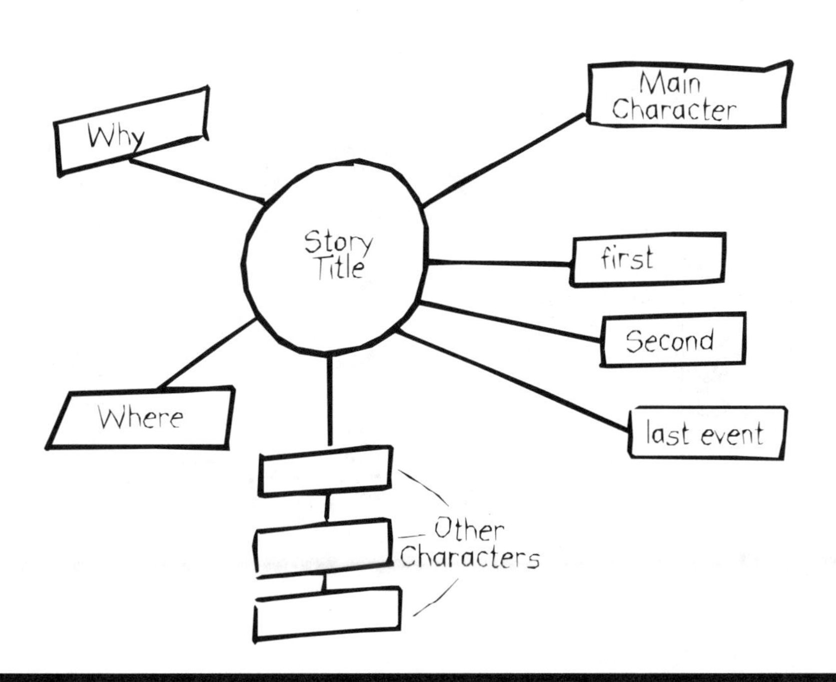

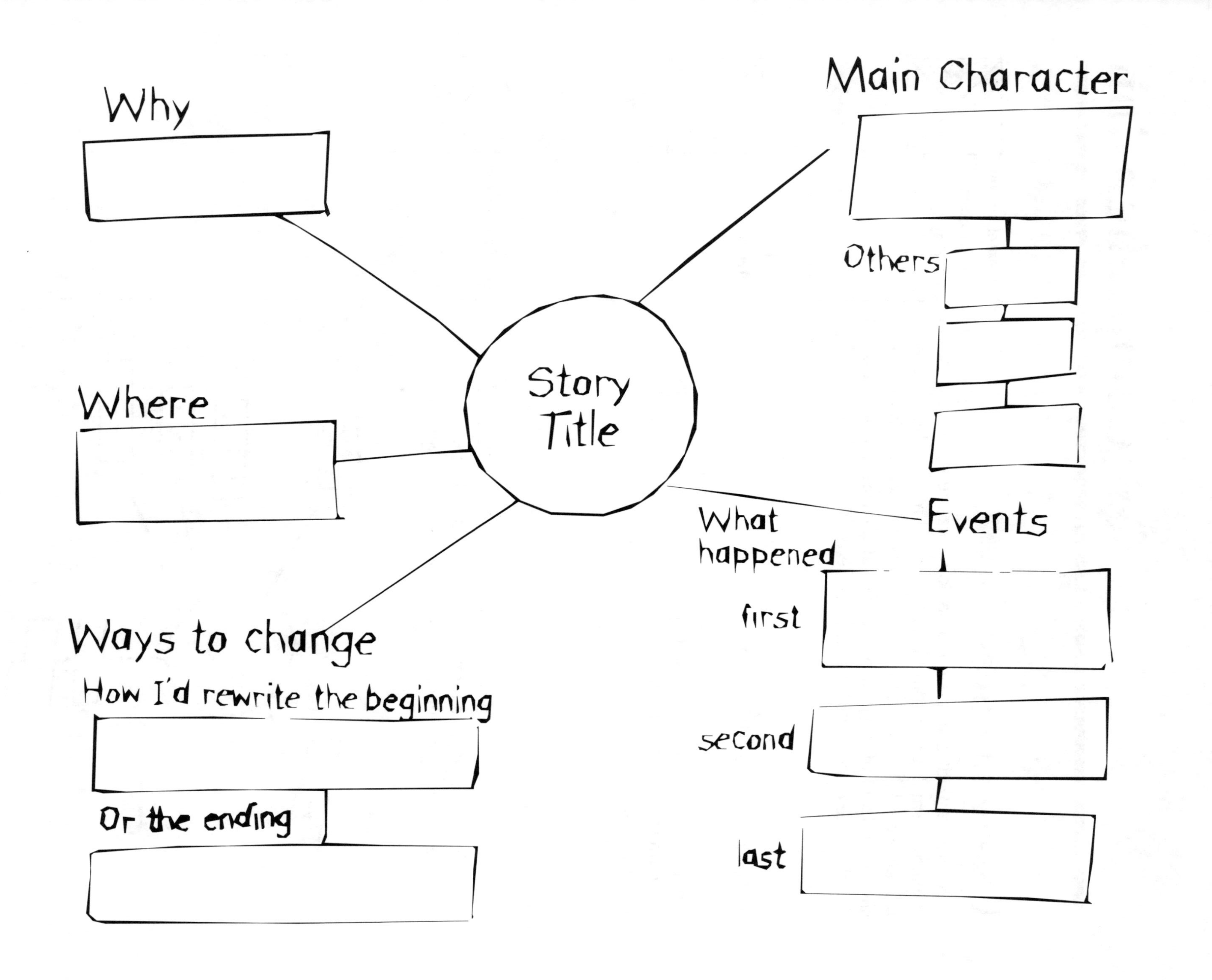
Story Title
Main Character
Others
Events
What happened
first
second
last
Why
Where
Ways to change
How I'd rewrite the beginning
Or the ending

MORE Comprehension

Pass the Hat

While reading a story to the class, have the students pass a special hat, tiara, or paper crown around the class. Stop reading suddenly; the student holding the hat must put the hat on her head and predict what happens next in the story.

predicting
retelling

Yes/No Comprehension Cards

On the left side of the inside of a file folder, write statements from an assigned story. On the right side of the folder, write the words "Yes" and "No" across from each statement. Write an answer key on the back of the folder, and laminate the folder. Students answer each question by circling "yes" or "no," then check their work by looking at the answer key.

comprehension

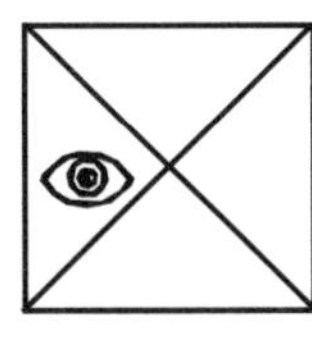

Name that Tune

Teach a simple tune to the class; the tunes from the songs "Row, Row, Row Your Boat" and "If You're Happy and You Know It" are good ones to use. After the children finish reading a story, have them sing or chant a summary of the story to the "class tune."

book reviews

book reviews

Crossword Puzzles

Use this to test comprehension instead of worksheets. Write questions and answers about a story the students have read; place the answers into a crossword grid. Trace around the grid, and distribute the blank, numbered grids to the students along with the questions.

Across:

1. What was Joey's dog's name?
2. What did Joey forget?

Down:

1. How did Joey get to the store?
3. What did Joey buy?

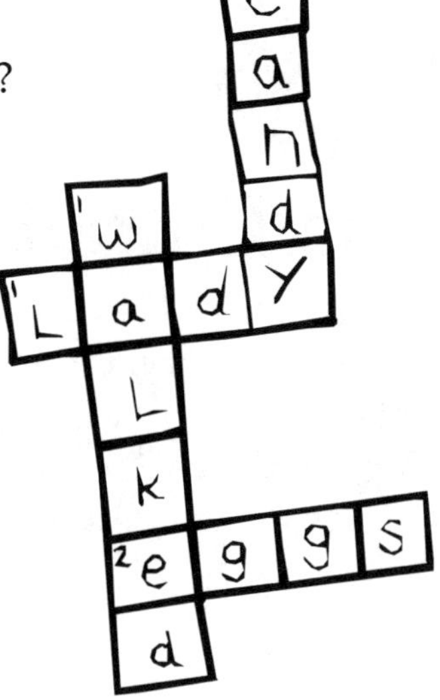

higher-level thinking

Cause and Effect Tag

Divide the class into two-person teams. Give one member of each team a sentence or phrase which describes an event in the story. The first person reads the sentence to his partner; his partner must finish it by saying *why* the event happened. For instance:

Shelley got her umbrella . . . because it was raining.

Dino got a bone . . . because he learned to roll over.

Team members can take turns giving events and reasons.

Playing for a Cause

cause and effect
oral sequencing

Ask students to bring in an old toy. Demonstrate the concept of cause and effect by using the toys:

The siren squeals . . . because the wheel turns when the car is pushed forward.

The balloon squeaks . . . because it has a leak.

The clown jumps from the Jack-in-the-Box . . . because the door opens, and the puppet is on a spring.

Jeopardy for Readers

oral expression

Use this activity to help students learn about "wh" questions. Design a game board, based on a particular story, with five columns of categories and five or more rows of answers. The child reveals the answer and then must ask the question that goes with the answer:

Category:	Pets
Answer:	Buster
Question:	Who was Ryan's dog?

Association Cards

sight words
memory

Use this game to help students associate a series of facts from given materials. Label twenty to thirty 3" x 5" cards with fact words, making sure that each card matches another card with an associated word.

Deal each child four cards. Place the rest of the deck of cards face down on the desk. As a child matches two or more cards based on their association with each other — for example, "shoe" and "sock," "dog," "collar," and "bone" — the child discards them by placing them face up beside the deck of unused cards, and drawing the same number of cards from the deck. The children continue to discard and take cards from the pile; the first child to lay down all of his cards is the winner.

MORE Comprehension

Toss for Association

Draw a hopscotch grid on the floor, or block it out with masking tape. Label each block of the grid with a specific category. Have students toss a coin or paper clip onto the grid; whichever block they land on, they must list as many items in that category as possible in twenty seconds.

Association Mix-Up

On different pieces of paper list three or four characters from each of several current movies or television shows (for example, Batman, Robin, and the Riddler; or Dino, Barney, and Betty).

Now list each of the characters on separate index cards. Distribute a card to each student. On a given signal, the students stand up and find the students with the matching cards. They must be prepared to discuss how and why the characters go together.

environmental print

Label Comprehension

Develop the concept of details by giving each student a candy wrapper, soup label, or vegetable label. Ask the children to "read to learn" by finding out how many ounces the candy bar weighs, what vegetables are included in the vegetable bag, etc.

Category Groups

association

After reading a story to the students, have them group the new vocabulary words from the story by category: things Timmy saw, where Billy traveled, etc.

Pop-Up Lollipops

sight words

Write vocabulary words or sight words on lollipop heads cut out of construction paper, and attach them to Popsicle sticks. On the lower portion of each Popsicle stick, draw a picture to match the word on the lollipop head. (You can also glue a cut-out picture onto the stick.) Put the lollipops in the can with only the word showing. As the student reads the word, she picks the lollipop out of the can to check the reading with the picture.

Apply the same idea to math facts; write the problems written on the lollipops and the answers on the sticks.

Frozen Vocabulary

sight words
definitions

Try this chilling approach to new vocabulary words. Cut five to ten ice cube shapes out of paper, and laminate them. On each cube, write a vocabulary word to be reinforced.

Have the students sit in a circle. Start passing an ice cube around the circle while playing a winter song on the tape player. Stop the music suddenly. Whoever is holding the cube must read the word aloud, define it, and use it in a sentence. If the student needs assistance, he may ask for help from the student on his left or right. If the student gives the correct answer, that cube is put aside and another cube is started around the circle.

association
sight words

CATegories

Write a list of words on a large cutout of a cat. Write the appropriate category for those words on the tail of the cat, and put the cat in a brown paper bag. Tell the students that the cat will slowly be let out of the bag. They must read the words on the cat as they appear and decide what the CATegory is before the cat is let out of the bag.

association
sight words
matching

Chug-a-Lug

Create two identical sets of word flash cards. Appoint one student as the conductor; make the game more interesting by having that student wear a conductor's cap.

Give the conductor one set of the word cards, and distribute the other set of cards to the students playing the game. The group sings their "choo-choo" chant, moving their arms to the chant. The conductor holds up one of her word cards and announces, "Whistle stop!" The students stop their choo-choo chant, and the student with the card matching the conductor's card says the word and uses it in a sentence. If the student is correct, he hands the card over to the conductor. The group continues to play the game until all the cards are handed in to the conductor.

Use this game as a math activity by having the conductor hold up a number; the train passengers must match the number with a corresponding fact card.

To review spelling, have the conductor hold up a definition card; the passenger matches it to her spelling word, spells it, and uses it in a sentence.

MORE Comprehension

sight words

Vocabulary Keys

Ask your local locksmith to save key rejects for you. Attach five to ten keys to silver notebook rings; create enough so each child can have one. Write one new vocabulary word on each key with a marker. When the children have mastered a word, remove the key and add a new word to the key ring.

sight words
definitions

Don't Talk Like That!

Divide the class into pairs to review new vocabulary words. Give one student a word card. She must define and describe the word to her partner without saying what the word is: "It's a large dinosaur; it flies. It lived long ago and is called ____________." Her partner must guess the word.

sight words
book reviews

Memory

After covering a topic or reading a story in class, choose a child from the class to experience amnesia. Have that child sit in the class rocking chair, facing away from his classmates. Hold up a vocabulary word from the unit of study you have just completed, making sure your "amnesia victim" can't see the word. The child's classmates must feed him clues to see if they can help the student guess the correct term.

Directional Reading

Write silly directions in each box of a game format or grid. Have the children use dice or a spinning needle, and count to a given space, or have them toss a coin or paper clip onto the box. They must read and follow the directions written on the box. (Examples: "Count backwards from one hundred to five by fives;" "Skip around the room twice;" "Crow three times."

Vocabulary Chain Letters

memory

Write vocabulary words from today's story on index cards or circle chips. Spread the cards/chips on a table or clip them onto the bulletin board. (Make sure every student can see all of the cards.) Call on one student to choose a word and use it in a sentence. The next student chooses another card and uses that word in a sentence to build onto the first student's sentence.

Prefix/Suffix Bingo

vocabulary
sight words

Write a prefix or suffix on each side of a cardboard cube. (You can make these cubes easily out of a coffee mug box.)

Make Bingo cards containing nineteen words and a free space. Appoint one student to roll the cube and call out the prefix which lands on top. If a student has a root word that can be attached to that prefix, he covers the word with a Bingo chip. The first child to cover a row wins and becomes the new caller.

MORE Comprehension

vocabulary
sight words

Super Suffixes

Cut a large piece of oak tag into 3" x 9" strips. Cut a 2" x 2" window in the right side of each strip. Write a base word on the left side of each strip, and a list of matching suffixes on a 2" x 6" piece of paper.

Have a student read the base word on the strip along with each of the suffixes on the list.

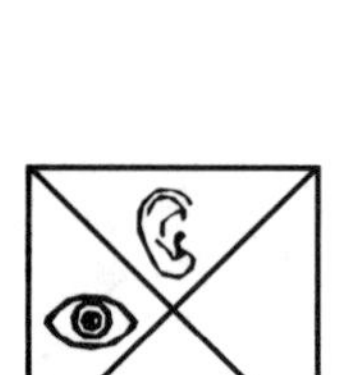

sight words
vocabulary

Antonym/Synonym Bingo

Distribute blank Bingo cards to each student. Create a set of index cards with all the words you want to review. Before the game, review these words with the students, and have them write a synonym (or antonym) for each word in a spot on the Bingo cards. Collect and redistribute the cards and begin the Bingo game.

vocabulary
sight words
dictionary skills

Mix-Ups

On 5" x 8" index cards, write vocabulary words and definitions; write the word on the left side of the card and the definition on the right. Cut apart the cards in jigsaw puzzle fashion, mix them up, and have the student match each word to its definition.

Group Tic Tac Toe

vocabulary
sight words
dictionary skills

Create and laminate a large tic tac toe grid. Write a vocabulary word in each section of the grid.

Divide the students into two teams. Announce a definition for one of the words. Give each team a turn to identify the vocabulary words: a player from Team One comes to the grid and puts an X on the word he thinks matches the definition. If he is right, leave the X; if not, erase it and give Team Two a turn. (Team Two writes an O.) The next definition goes first to Team Two. The first team to get three marks in a row wins.

The same activity can be adapted for addition facts and spelling definitions.

What a Cover-Up

vocabulary
sight words
dictionary skills

Before reading an assigned text, write each new vocabulary word from the text on individual index cards. On the back of each card, have the students write or illustrate the definition.

Place the vocabulary cards on the floor with the words face down and the definitions showing. As the teacher calls out a word, the student covers the definition with her foot.

Bean-O

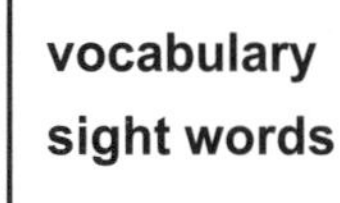

vocabulary
sight words

Use dry lima beans for this activity. Write a sight word to be reviewed on each bean with a fine-tipped marker. Place five to ten beans in an empty film container.

Divide the students into pairs. Have one student shake his can of beans out onto the table. The other team member must read each word, define it, and use it in a sentence.

This activity also lends itself well to individualized review; create a different canister for each student and put the students' names on their canisters.

MORE Comprehension

alphabetical order
dictionary skills
letters/sounds

My Own Pictionary

Purchase a blank scrapbook or bind your own, using twenty-six pages. Use a Hefty Tab or marker to mark each page with a different letter.

Give each student a catalog or magazine; as he finds pictures that he can identify as beginning with a certain letter, he can cut out the picture and paste it onto the appropriate page.

dictionary skills
letter formation

My Backwards Pictionary

For more fun, make the same kind of pictionary as above, but assemble it so that it opens from back to front. The students use this backwards pictionary the same way, except that they paste pictures into the book that *end* with each letter.

sight words
letter recognition

The Daily Sun

Give each student a piece of newspaper. Ask the students to circle all the words they can read on the page. Have them connect the circles and see what picture they have created.

Some students can use this activity for letter recognition instead of word recognition.

Footprint Fantasy

vocabulary
sight words
alphabetical order

Put a small amount of tempera paint in a dishpan. Have each student dip her bare foot into the paint, then put her foot on the center of a piece of construction paper.

Once the footprints are dry, laminate them and place them on the floor around the room. Write words like "beginning," "middle," and "end" and have the students "walk" the parts of a story; or write vocabulary words and have students step on each word they can use in a sentence.

More Mix-Ups

blending
decoding

Use two shoe boxes for this activity. On index cards, write all the consonants of the alphabet, as well as a variety of letter blends, and put them into the first box. In the second box place a selection of word families — it, at, en, op, im, us. The students pick the beginning letter or blend out of the first box, choose a family from the second box, blend the sounds, and decide if the result is a "real" word.

Here's the Scoop

blending
decoding
sight words

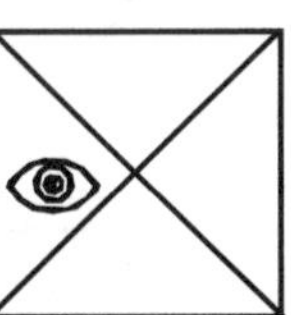

Create paper ice cream cones and scoops of ice cream. Have the students match cones and scoops to practice matching vowel sounds to words, combining words to create compound words, matching words to definitions, etc.

If you laminate the pieces before you write on them you can wipe off the lettering and reuse them for a variety of activities.

MORE Comprehension

contractions

Apple of My Eye

Trace a picture of an apple onto red construction paper; cut a variety of worms out of green or brown construction paper.

Write contractions on the apples; write the two words that make up each contraction on the worms. The student must attach the right worm to the right apple. Write the answer on the back of each apple for self-checking.

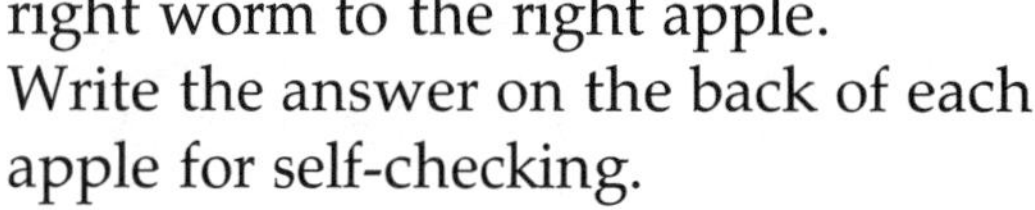

compound words

auditory comprehension

Compounded Chains

Divide the students into small groups for this activity.

Have the first member of each group write a compound word on a 3" x 5" index card; for example, "downtown." The student then passes the card to the student on his left, who must take the last word in the compound word ("town") and use it as the first word in a new compound word ("townhouse"). The index card gets passed around the group until no one can think of a new word to be formed.

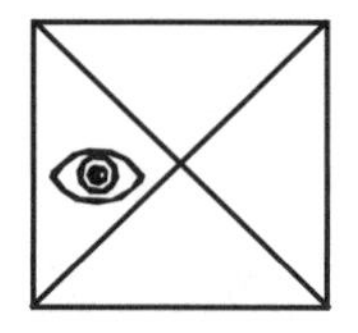

memory

comprehension

Compounding Concentration

List twenty different compound words on a sheet of paper. Now write each part of the compound word on a separate index card. Place the forty index cards face down, eight in a row, five rows each. Have a student turn over two cards. If the words on those cards can be put together to form a compound word, the student keeps the two cards and earns a point. If the two words cannot be joined into a compound word, the cards are turned over and the next student gets a turn.

Hear Thyself

Have a child read a passage or story into a tape recorder, then play back the recording and follow along in his book as he listens to himself read. Discuss the passage with the child, and talk about the concept of fluency.

oral expression
comprehension

Hear Thy Helper

Sit close to a child's nondominant hand and read aloud to the child at an appropriate pace as the child follows along in the book. This will help increase speed and fluency.

oral
expression

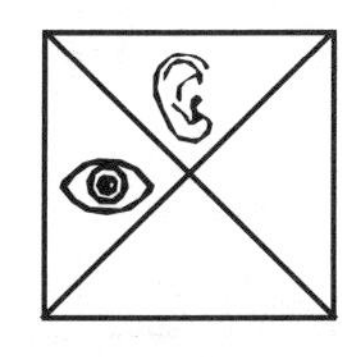

Trackers

Purchase a plastic paw or finger from a novelty shop. (These are easy to find at Halloween.) The children can use these paws or fingers for visual tracking.

visual tracking

MORE Fluency

Flash cards

Create phrase flash cards based on a story you have read to the class. Use these phrase flash cards for review instead of word flash cards to help students develop the skill of reading phrases rather than word by word.

motivation

Flip Flop Fluency

Create different sets of flash cards at different reading levels for use with individual students.

Fold a piece of paper in half. Label one half of the paper "Flip" and the other half "Flop." Hold up a flash card and have the student read the card. If she reads the card fluently, she gets a tally under "Flip." If she cannot read the card, or stumbles over the word, she gets a "Flop." This is a good way for students to individually measure their progress.

comprehension

Zip Up the Sentences

On a strip of paper, write a complete sentence; cut the sentence apart by individual words and put the sentence in a Ziploc bag. The student must empty the bag and reassemble the sentence.

Create a different bag for each student, geared toward the child's reading level.

Top It Off

Use this folder activity to practice identifying the main topic of an article or story. Gather short stories or paragraphs from the students' readers. Glue the articles to the front of a file folder.

Have the student read the article and write the main topic of the paragraph inside the folder. Provide an answer key on the back of the folder.

Adapt this activity for some students by creating multiple choice answers on the inside of the folder.

comprehension
main idea

MORE Book Reviews

comprehension
main idea

Time Capsules

Create a time capsule in your classroom in a large coffee can or cardboard treasure chest.

After students finish reading a book, have them place artifacts from the book inside individual Ziploc bags. For instance, if they've read *Willie Wonka,* a student might place a chocolate bar in his bag. Place the Ziploc bags in the time capsule.

At the end of each month, pull a bag from the container and ask the student who contributed it to describe its contents and their significance.

oral expression
role play

Interviews

After reading a story to the students, divide them into pairs and encourage them to set up television interviews for their favorite characters. One student can be the interviewer and the other student the main character in the story. If possible, videotape the interviews and play them back in class, both for the students' enjoyment and for visitors.

comprehension
main idea
main characters

Wearable Review Shirts

After finishing an assigned book, have the students each design a T-shirt representinga character from the story. Use iron-on crayons or puff paints for interesting designs.

MORE Book Reviews

Bag It

comprehension
higher-level thinking

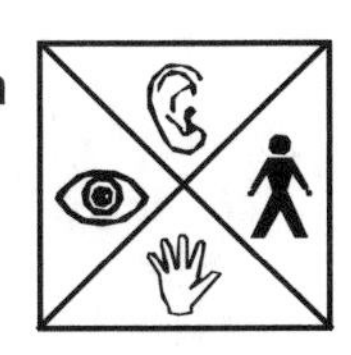

Purchase inexpensive paper gift bags with handles. Decorate the front of each bag with a picture or scene from a favorite grade-level book. Inside each bag place a paperback copy of the book, and two or three activity cards hooked together on a silver notebook ring. When a student chooses to read that book, ideas for activities are already included with the book.

Potent Posies

main idea
comprehension

Cut a 4" circle out of oak tag, and write the name of a book on the center circle. Attach petal facts describing the book to the center circle.

For children who have difficulty writing details, have them draw the parts of their book review, or pair them off with a reading buddy and allow them to dictate the facts to their buddy.

Playing Post Office

summarizing
written expression

Ask parents to supply their child with nine stamped postcards to bring to class. Address the postcards to special school friends, including the principal, the nurse, the guidance counselor, and other classroom teachers. Each month the children will read a book of their choice, pick an addressed post card, write a brief summary of the book, and mail the news to their special friend.

MORE Book Reviews

parts of a story

written expression

Wrap It Up

After completing a book, help the students wrap up the story. Cut oak tag into 6" x 24" strips. Fold each strip into thirds to create a little book. The different parts of the book represent the beginning, middle, and end of the story.

Beginning | Middle | End

Attach a colorful ribbon to the outside of the book, so that when the strip is folded, the ribbon can be tied to keep the book closed. Distribute the books. The students can untie the ribbons, open up the books, and design the three parts of the book as they wish. After they've finished their books, they can tie them together again and share them with other students in the class.

parental involvement

comprehension

written/oral expression

Family Bag It

Create these bags to send home with the children. In a large Ziploc freezer bag, place a book, a taped version of the story (so younger members of the family can enjoy the story), and a week's worth of activities.

For example:

Monday	Read *Mrs. Wishy Washy.* Listen to the tape.
Tuesday	Help someone in your home wash the dishes.
Wednesday	Use soap and water to wash two of your favorite toys. Make sure you have a grown-up's permission.
Thursday	Help separate the wash for your family.
Friday	Practice writing your spelling words in soap on the wall of the tub.

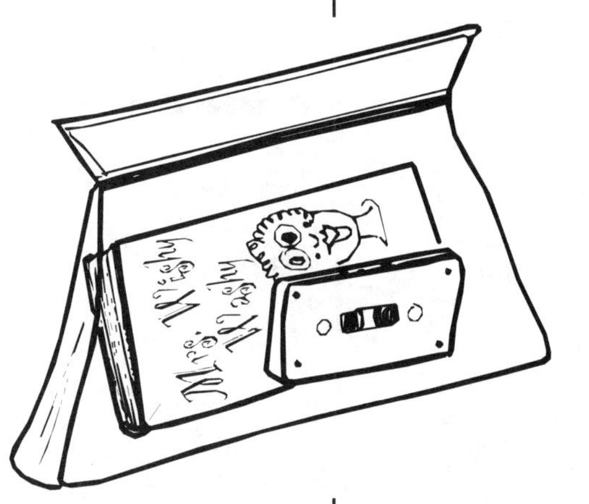

Main Character Poems

Instruct the students to write the character's name, letter by letter, down the side of a page. Have them write a poem about the character, using the letters of the character's name as the beginning letters in each line of poetry.

Arthur, friendly and nice
Reads to his friends
Thanks his teacher
Helps his father
Understands differences
Remembers what learning is

poetry
written expression
comprehension

Review Corners

Write out review statements about a book the children have finished reading. For instance, after completing *Charlotte's Web,* you might write the statements:

> "Charlotte is portrayed as a very weak character."
>
> "Wilbur could have best been described by having him be a cat."

Create a poster out of oak tag, labeling the four corners with the statements:

> "I agree because . . ."
>
> "I disagree because . . ."
>
> "I would have . . ."
>
> "The author could have . . ."

Hang the poster up in the front of the room.

Read the review statements to the class; have the children stand in the corner of the room which represents their opinion based on the poster, and discuss their opinions, using the opinion statements as the beginning of their responses.

oral expression
higher-level thinking
comprehension

MORE Sequencing

oral
expression

How-To

Buy a children's "How to Draw" book with step-by-step illustrations of the drawing projects in the book. (You can find these inexpensive books, such as *How to Draw Farm Animals, How to Draw Cats,* etc., at most local bookstores.) Cut the sequenced pictures apart and paste them onto index cards. Number the pictures on the backs of the cards according to the proper sequence. Have the students recreate the proper sequence, explain their response orally, then check themselves by looking at the back of the cards.

alphabetical
order

before and
after

Before and After Bingo

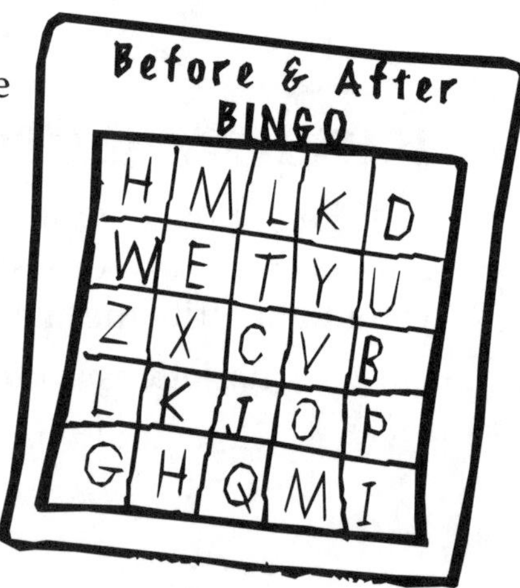

Pass out blank Bingo grids and ask the students to write one letter in each of the boxes in the grid. Have the students pass their completed grids two people to the right.

Appoint one child to be "it." The child's job is to hold up a letter card, "B," for example, for the children to see. The child who is "it" asks the rest of the students to cover the square containing the letter after "B" in the alphabet. When one child's entire grid is covered, that student becomes the caller.

alphabetical
order

sight words

ABC Line-Up

Tape an alphabet strip across the top of the inside of a file folder. Write numbers from 1 to 10 down the left side of the folder. Give the child the folder, and have him draw words and pictures from this week's reading or theme unit in the right order alphabetically.

Hanging around the ABC's

alphabetical order

letter sounds

String a clothesline across the back of the room; hang the letters of the alphabet on the line with pinch clothespins. Have each child search through catalogs or magazines to find a favorite picture, then hang his picture on the line next to the corresponding letter.

ABC Light-Ups

letter sounds

parental involvement

Punch the form of a letter of the alphabet in a 5" x 8" index card using a hole punch. Place the punched-out letter on the overhead projector. As its holey outline is flashed onto the screen, the children can identify the letter or draw a picture of something that begins with that letter.

Bag It

letter recognition

Assign one letter of the alphabet a week. Send Ziploc sandwich bags home to parents; ask the parents to help their child collect one or two items beginning with the assigned letter to put into the sandwich bag and bring back to school. Write each word represented by the items in the Ziploc bags on a large piece of chart paper; while you're writing the word, encourage the children to pin their bags next to the word on the chart. (Since there may be more than one item in each bag, some children will have to move their bags to more than one word.)

Writing Adaptations

General Adaptations

SQUIWT

Have a special class time called SQUIWT — Sustained Quiet UnInterrupted Writing Time (rhymes with 'twit'). If the teacher calls out "SQUIWT" anytime during the day, students pull out folders and begin to write.

Use the same technique with SQUIRT — Sustained Quiet UnInterrupted Reading Time.

organization

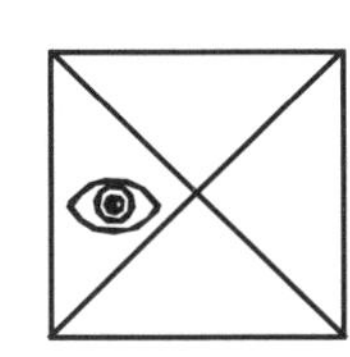

Don't Forget

Cover textbooks with oilcloth or plain brown bags, or laminate the book covers. Encourage students to write their nightly homework right on the book's cover. Wipe off or erase at the end of each week.

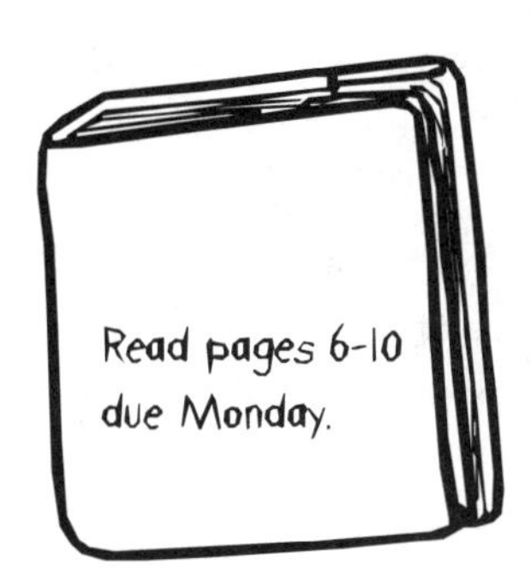

Self-Identification

Glue yearbook-sized pictures of the students onto index cards or "Hello" tags. Encourage each student to create his own ID tag including his name, address, phone number, height, weight, and parents' names.

organization
self-awareness

Toss Up

Toss this cube to decide whose turn it is to have a writing conference or to share writing with the class.

Laminate the sides of a cube, or cover it with acetate. Write a number on each side of the cube, based on the number of letters in the participating students' names. Match the students' names to the number that comes up when you toss the cube. If more than one student has the same number of letters in their names, have a toss off: each student tosses the cube, and the one with the highest number takes her turn first. (See cube pattern on page 77.)

James=5
Alex=4
Joanna=6
Tom=3
Joe=3

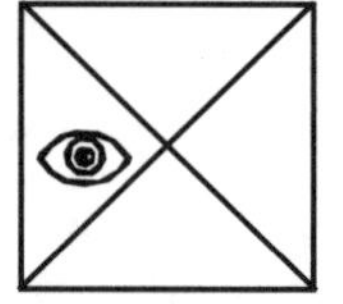

organization

Colorful Flash Cards

Color-code flash cards by ability level; students who need simpler tasks choose from one color, students with more advanced skills from another.

Clipboard

organization
self-awareness

Create a color key based on the steps in the writing process: rough draft, editing, typing, illustration, and sharing.

List each student's name horizontally on a chart made from a narrow piece of oak tag. Punch a hole under each student's name. As the students move through the steps in publishing, have them hook a color-coded clip or ring underneath their names. This way, you can see at a glance where each child is in the writing process.

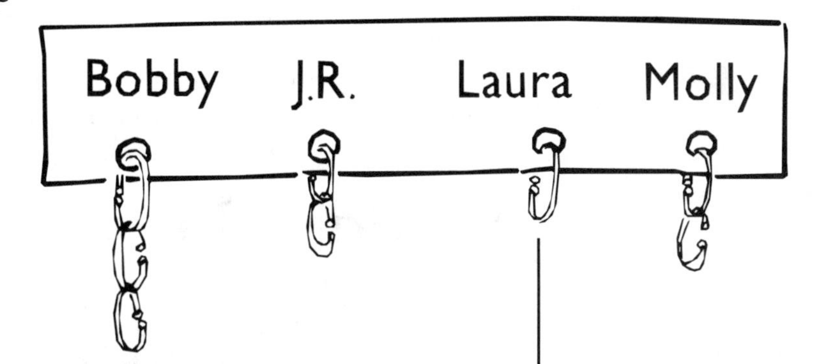

Wrapped-Up Writing

organization

Create a scroll by gluing a straw to each end of a piece of 5" x 10" white paper. Have the students write and illustrate a sentence or a short story on the scrolls. Roll the straws toward the center, and tie the scrolls shut with gold ribbon. Store the scrolls in a candy jar or fancy box and use them during reading, writing, and sharing times.

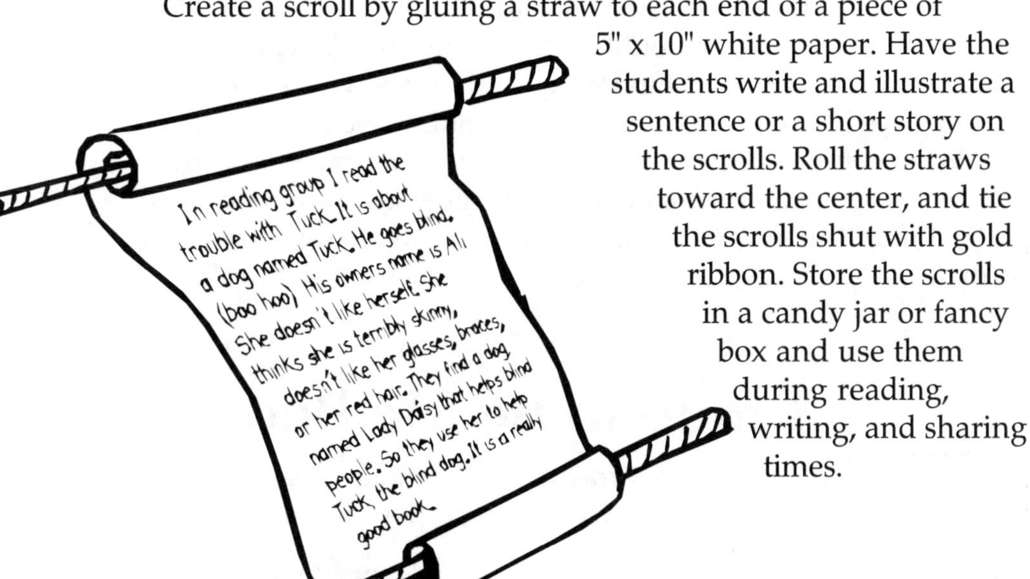

Birthday Book

On each child's birthday, ask the class to prepare a birthday book for the student. Have each class member write a page of positive things about the birthday student; the teacher then binds the book together. Appoint one student to create a cover for the book.

The younger students may need a leading sentence such as, "I like Shari because_________." or "Shari is a good friend because_________."

For children whose birthdays fall on a vacation day, designate a different day for each child as a pretend birthday.

Surprise Box

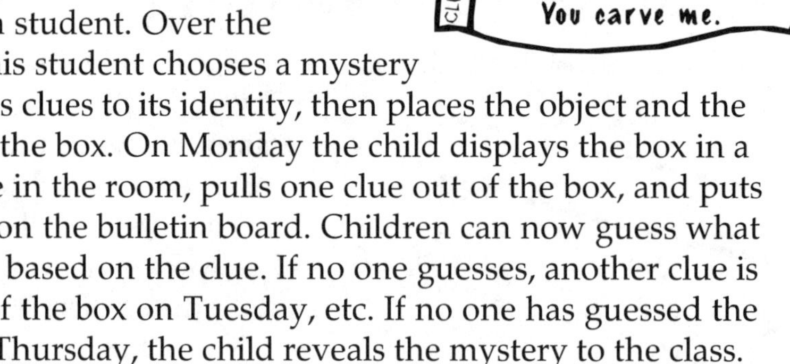

Turn a lidded tin box (like the ones Christmas cookies come in) into a surprise box. Every Friday, send the box home with a student. Over the weekend, this student chooses a mystery object, writes clues to its identity, then places the object and the clues inside the box. On Monday the child displays the box in a special place in the room, pulls one clue out of the box, and puts the clue up on the bulletin board. Children can now guess what is in the box based on the clue. If no one guesses, another clue is pulled out of the box on Tuesday, etc. If no one has guessed the surprise by Thursday, the child reveals the mystery to the class.

self-awareness

Proud to Be Me Book

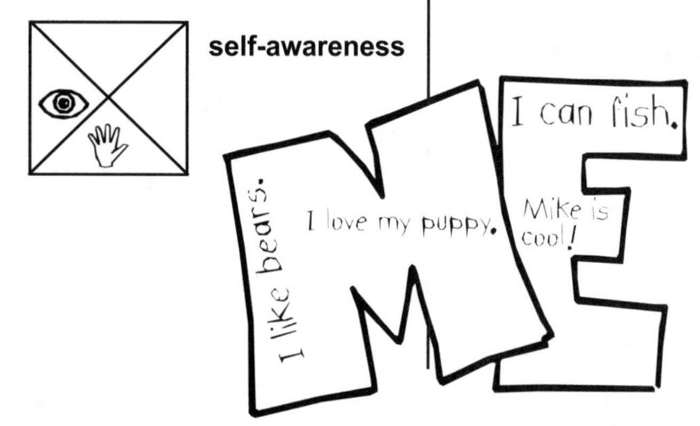

Cut the word "ME" out of heavy oak tag or poster board. Give each student his own ME.

Allow the students to decorate and write descriptive phrases about themselves to help peers learn who they really are. Bind the ME pages together for a handy classroom directory.

MORE Acceptance and Self-Esteem

Postcards from the Pad

parental involvement

Ask each parent or caregiver to complete a picture postcard* containing information about her child, and mail the postcard to school. As the postcards are received, display them on the bulletin board.

Warm Fuzzies

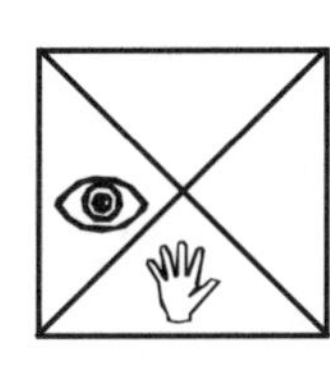

Have each student write his name on a Popsicle stick; put the sticks in a jar. Every Friday, have each student pull a name from the jar. For the next week, the students must secretly observe the classmate whose name they pulled, and document all random acts of kindness performed by that person. The students share the information they gather with each other at the end of the week.

Paired Bios

Have the children work in pairs and take turns interviewing their partner about their likes and dislikes, family history, strengths, and favorite books. Once the students have interviewed their partners, they must write a biography and read it to the class.

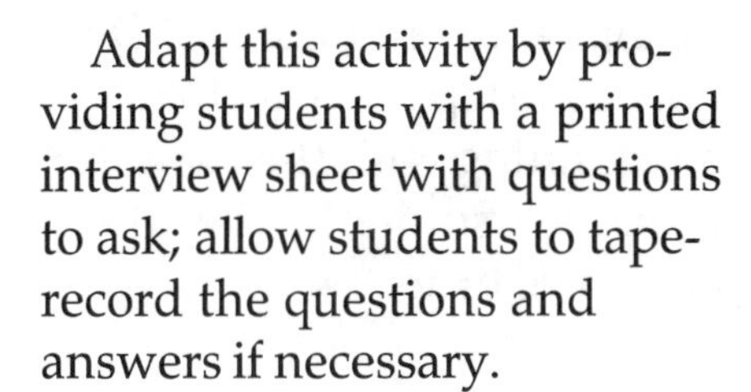

Adapt this activity by providing students with a printed interview sheet with questions to ask; allow students to tape-record the questions and answers if necessary.

* Local film processing centers can make postcards out of photos of your students to use with this activity. (A 4"x 6" photograph is the same size as a postcard.)

MORE Handwriting/Letter Recognition

Writing Letters

Choose four or five letters of the alphabet each week, and post them on the bulletin board. When you need an activity to fill a few minutes, ask the children to write a sentence using all four letters. For example:

ABCD = Always Buy Cream Doughnuts.

sequencing

Staircase to Z

Create a large cutout of a staircase with 13 steps. Write two letters on the top of each step, in alphabetical order — AB, CD, EF, etc., until you've written the whole alphabet on the steps. On the vertical part of each step, have a child write two words beginning with the two letters on the step. Make sure the student writes the words in the correct alphabetical order.

AB animal bat
CD cat dog
EF egg flop
GH girl house

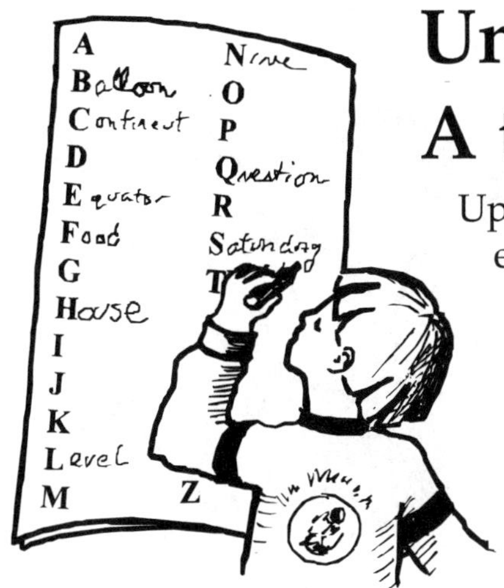

Unit Review from A to Z

sequencing
memory
review

Upon completing a thematic unit, hand each student a piece of paper with the alphabet written along the side. Have the students see how many words from the unit they can recall beginning with each letter.

My Boo-Boo Body Book

self-awareness

This whole-group activity is a fun way to review the names of body parts. Create blank books with about twelve pages each: stack four pieces of paper together and fold the stack in half; staple or bind the pages in the middle. Give one of these blank books to each child in the class.

Ask each student to draw a picture of her eye on the first page of her book. Tape the word "eye" onto the chalkboard. On the next page have each student draw a mouth, etc. Continue with different body parts until the book is full.

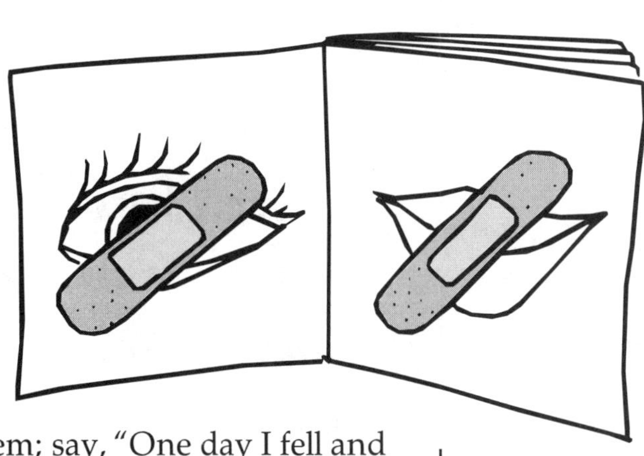

Now distribute 12 Band-Aids to each child. Beginning at the first page, model your instructions for them; say, "One day I fell and hurt my______." Each student must put a Band-Aid on the eye drawing and write the word "eye" on the page.

MORE Punctuation

Clip It On

Write a selection of sentences on laminated sentence strips; omit the punctuation marks. Write a variety of punctuation marks on clip-on clothes-pins.

The students clip the correct punctuation marks in the right places on each sentence strip. Write the answers on the backs of the sentence strips for self-checking.

Live Punctuation

Write the sentence you are reviewing in big letters on the chalkboard. Have several children each wear a sign with one of the necessary punctuation marks: an apostrophe, comma, period, etc. The children must bring the punctuation to life by standing in front of the sentence in the right place.

Punctuation

Punctuation Spinners

Try this activity for sentence review. Divide a large paper plate into four sections. Attach a spinner to the center. The student spins the dial and is asked to write a specific sentence. For some students who may need extra practice, they could be encouraged to match a sentence card to that specific type of sentence.

Punctuation Bingo

Distribute laminated Bingo grids to each student. Have the students place a punctuation mark in each square of the grids. Pass the grids to the right. Appoint one student to read a variety of sentences to the class. The students cross off the correct punctuation marks with a marker. The first to cross off all the marks becomes the next caller.

MORE Sentence Structure

Pocket Sentences

Glue three library pockets along the top of an open file folder. Color-code each pocket; create phrase strips and color-code them. Have the students choose one card from each pocket and assemble a sentence. Mix them up and try again.

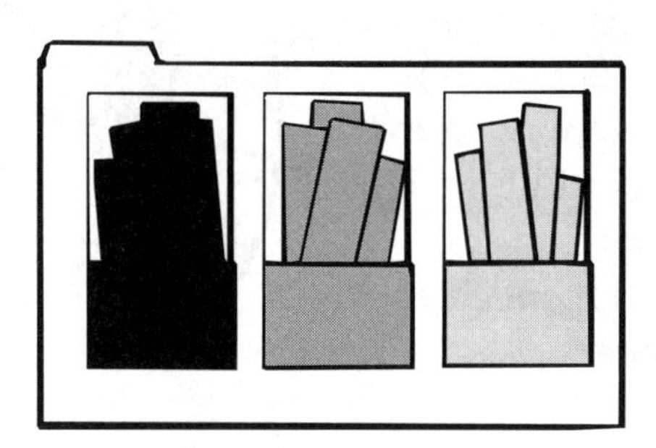

Dialing a Sentence

Use a large cutout of a rotary phone. Attach a phrase to each number of the dial. The student must dial one phrase, then another, and read and write the funny sentence she has just "called up."

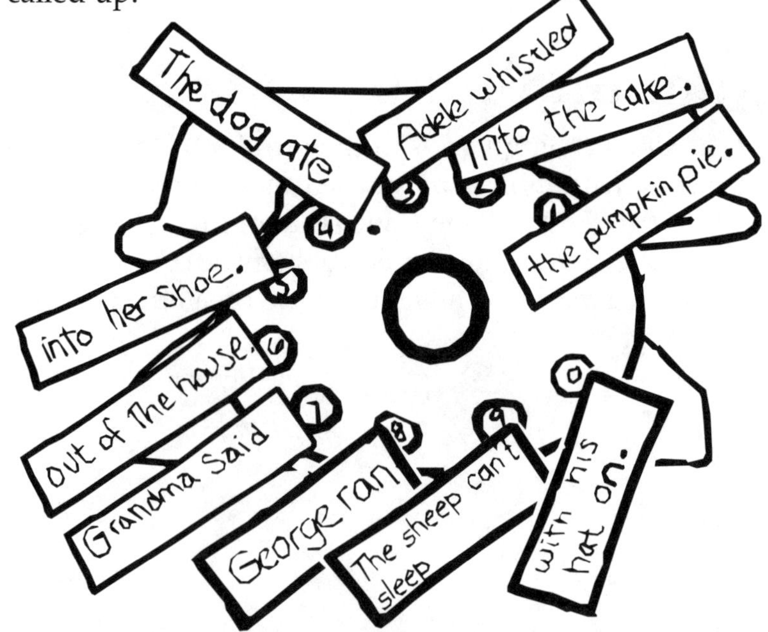

Adjective Crazies

Introduce older students to the concept behind "mad-lib" books, then have them write their own paragraphs using as many adjectives as possible. Instruct the students to go back over their completed paragraphs and erase the adjectives, replacing them with numerals beginning with "1".

On a separate piece of paper, list the same numerals. Have one of the students write an adjective beside each numeral. Now the students must go back over their paragraphs, replacing each numeral with the assigned adjectives. The students can now read their paragraphs to the class, and see how their stories have changed.

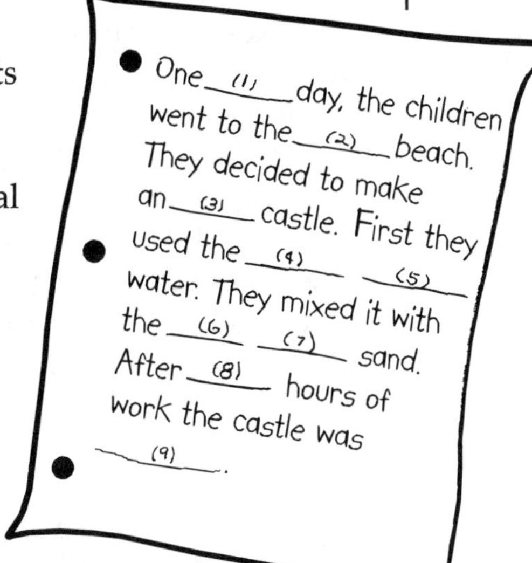

Fill in the Missing Loops

Provide the class or small group with a loop drawing. Have a child write a word in the first loop. The next child must write a word that goes with the first word in the second loop, and so on until all of the loops are filled. Make sure that the last word matches the word in the first loop.

apples
red
shiny
yummy
sweet
good
tart

MORE Adjectives

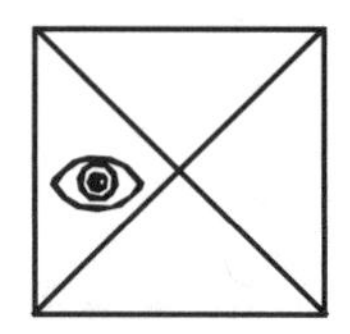

Wrap It Up Word Bank

To encourage students to use the most descriptive words possible in their writing, wrap two boxes in wrapping paper; cover one box with wrinkled brown paper, the other with beautiful wrapping paper. Keep ordinary adjectives — good, nice, pretty, okay — in the brown box; in the beautifully wrapped box keep more descriptive adjectives like kindhearted, exuberant, etc. Have the children pull adjectives out of the pretty box to use when writing.

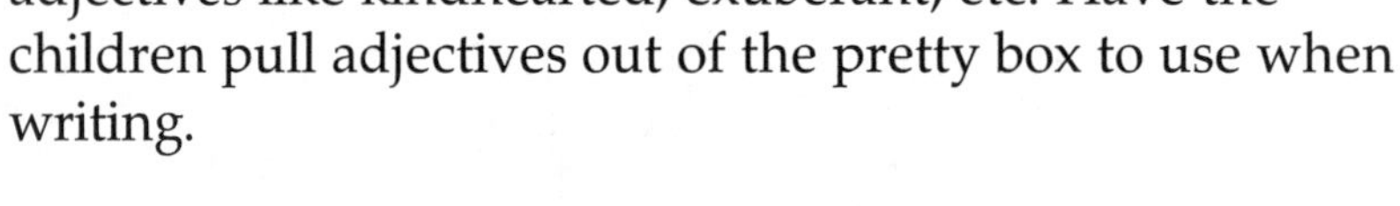

Edible Adjectives

Try this delicious homework assignment: each child places one piece of a favorite snack in a brown lunch bag.* On the front of the bag, the student writes at least five adjectives to describe his surprise treat. The next day, the children take turns reading their adjectives to their classmates. The student who correctly guesses the treat inside the bag gets to eat the snack. (To make sure all children get to have a snack, have the students drop out of the game after they get a treat.)

Students who are less eager to participate can be partnered with more verbal students; in this instance, the team gets two chances to win a treat.

* Make sure you send a questionnaire about food allergies home to all parents. Notify parents of any allergies, not only for this activity, but for all class parties/celebrations as well.

Edible Adverbs

Pass a small Ziploc bag of goodies around the class.* Have each student choose one treat to eat; as they devour the food, they must write verbs and adverbs to describe their activity — chomping loudly, quietly unwrapping, biting carefully, etc.

* See previous page for caution about food allergies.

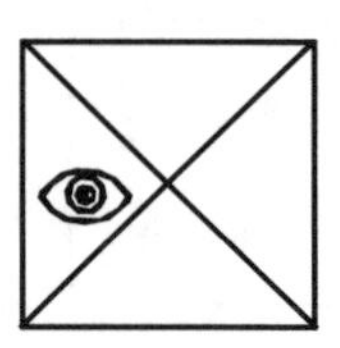

Venn Diagrams

Use a Venn diagram to help students understand categories and relationships. Select two words representing objects or ideas with similar characteristics. Show the students how to write characteristics in each circle; discuss which characteristics go in which circle, and which characteristics go in the overlapping circles.

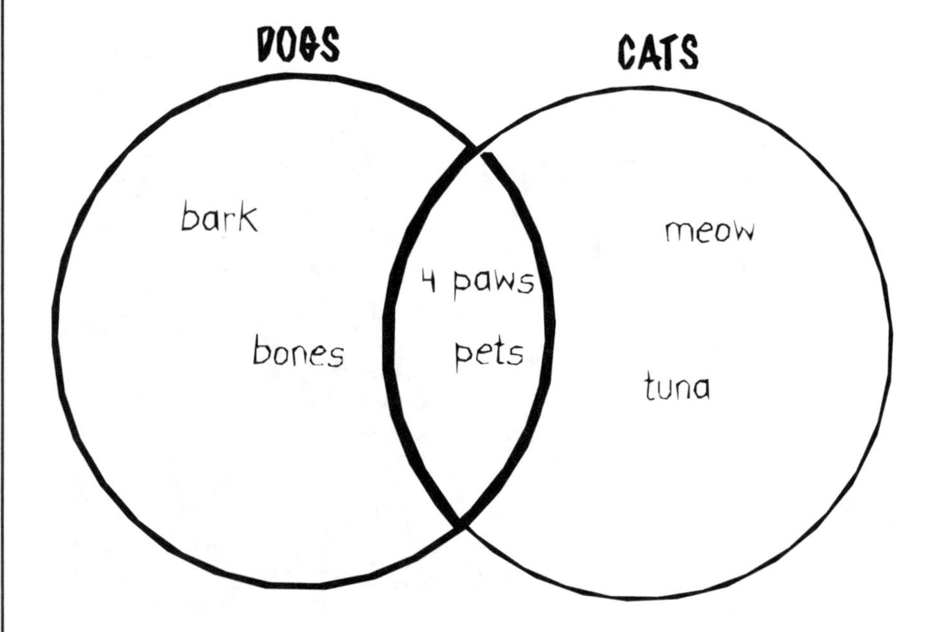

Post-It Words

Give each student a picture from a magazine or catalog, plus a pack of mini Post-It notes. The students must label as many parts of the picture as they can with the notes.

MORE Writing Ideas

creative expression

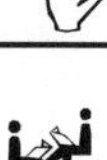

Springboard to Story Ideas

Create three sets of six index cards, using different colors for each set, listing individual ideas for character, setting, and plot. Number each set of cards from 1 to 6. Attach the sets of cards to a piece of oak tag with notebook rings or plastic spiral binders.

The student tosses a die and flips the first set of cards to the index card with that number, then does the same for the second and third sets. The student must take the character, setting, and plot ideas and combine them to create an oral or written story.

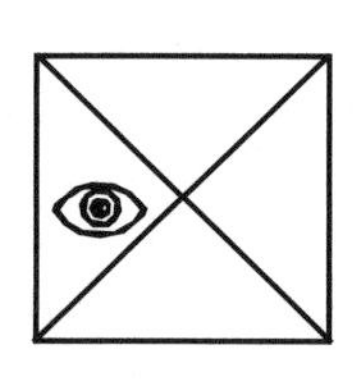

Photo Writing

For students who have a difficult time generating their own writing topics, hang a photo from a family album or a picture from a *National Geographic* magazine on the bulletin board as motivation.

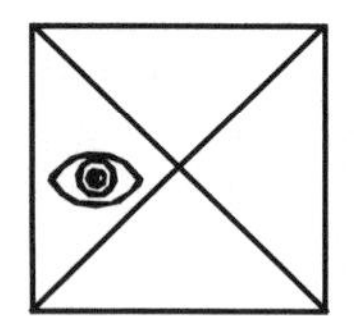

creative expression

parental involvement

Back-to-School Night

Place a blank school-year calendar on each child's desk for back-to-school night. Ask the parents to write at least two topic ideas, based on their child's real experiences, on each page of the calendar to motivate their child's writing. For example:

September	Helping my dad rake is so much fun, I can't wait until next fall.
December	How my life changed when a snowball went through Mrs. Smith's window.

Allow children who do not have parental support with schoolwork to take their calendars around the school to be filled in by support staff.

School Is Cool

creative expression
motivation

Have veteran students design and write advertisements for incoming students: Fold a piece of 9" x 12" construction paper into thirds, like a brochure. On the front of the brochure have students write a title: "Welcome to Room 203," or "The Things You'll Do While in Room 3b!" The students fill the inside of the brochure with exciting facts about their classroom.

Animal Adventures

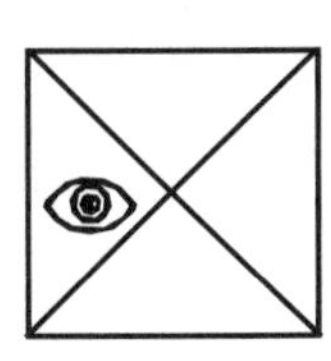

Cut color animal pictures from a magazine. Laminate the pictures. Clip each picture to a piece of writing paper. Have each student select an appealing picture and write a story to match.

Think Tank

Use an empty aquarium tank or fish bowl. Place cut-out fish in the tank. On each fish, write a story idea or other writing topic. When students are stumped for writing ideas, they can catch one from the tank. (Use fish patterns on page 68.)

MORE Writing Ideas

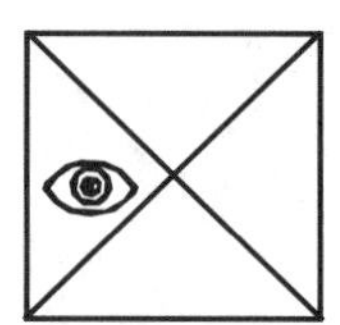

Put Yourself in My Shoes

Cut large outlines of shoes out of oak tag. Glue eye-catching pictures from a magazine or catalog to each shoe. Store the shoes in a shoe box. When the children are stuck for a writing topic, have them "put themselves in someone else's shoes" by picking a shoe and writing about the picture.

Tricks Are for Kids

Have parents save empty cereal boxes. Cut the front and back covers off the boxes and use them as story starters:

If Trix Weren't for Kids

The Day Cheerios Fell From the Sky

Use the covers to create durable front and back book covers for the stories.

Computer Label

Prepare a variety of computerized labels that contain messages such as:

What a great job I did!

One night the electricity blew up.

And so, never again will my life be the same.

Attach each label to a piece of paper; each student can pick a label and use it for a story lead-in or ending.

Post-It Words

Give each student a picture from a magazine or catalog, plus a pack of mini Post-It notes. The students must label as many parts of the picture as they can with the notes.

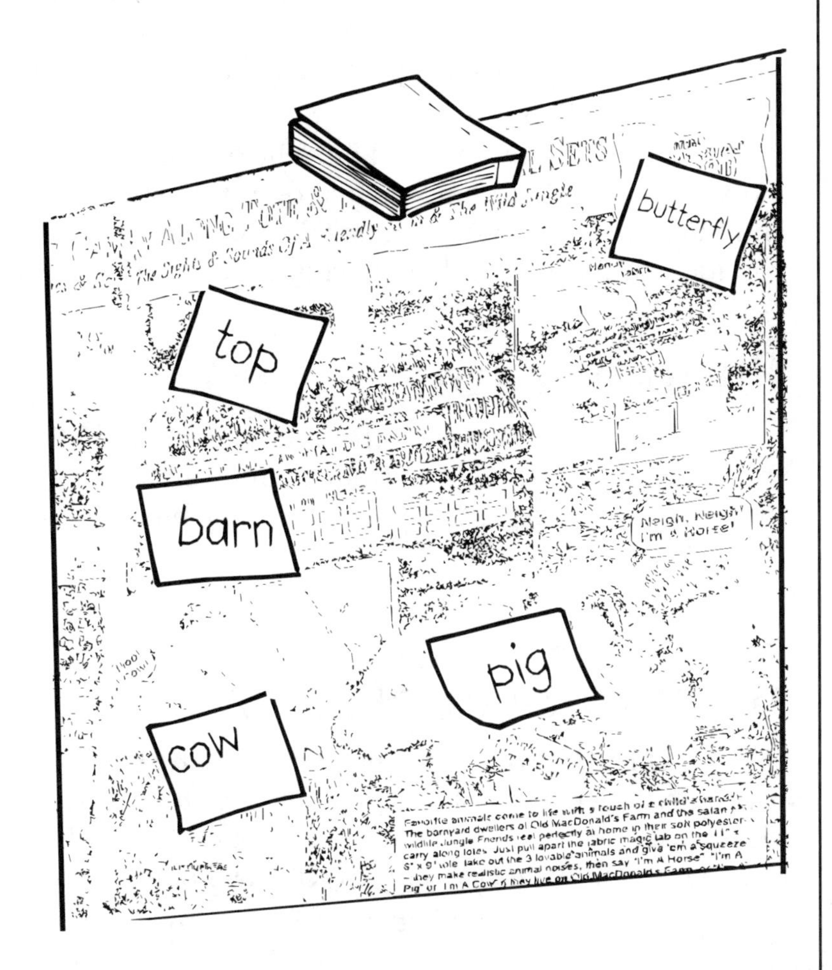

MORE Writing Ideas

creative expression

Springboard to Story Ideas

Create three sets of six index cards, using different colors for each set, listing individual ideas for character, setting, and plot. Number each set of cards from 1 to 6. Attach the sets of cards to a piece of oak tag with notebook rings or plastic spiral binders.

The student tosses a die and flips the first set of cards to the index card with that number, then does the same for the second and third sets. The student must take the character, setting, and plot ideas and combine them to create an oral or written story.

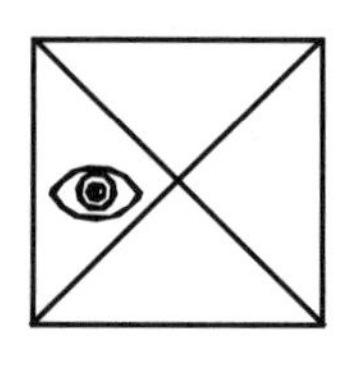

Photo Writing

For students who have a difficult time generating their own writing topics, hang a photo from a family album or a picture from a *National Geographic* magazine on the bulletin board as motivation.

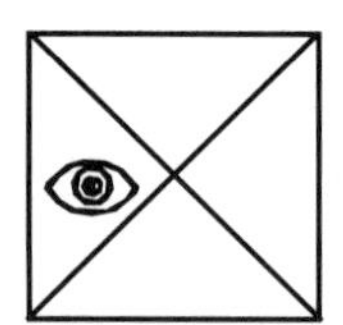

creative expression

parental involvement

Back-to-School Night

Place a blank school-year calendar on each child's desk for back-to-school night. Ask the parents to write at least two topic ideas, based on their child's real experiences, on each page of the calendar to motivate their child's writing. For example:

September	Helping my dad rake is so much fun, I can't wait until next fall.
December	How my life changed when a snowball went through Mrs. Smith's window.

Allow children who do not have parental support with schoolwork to take their calendars around the school to be filled in by support staff.

Critics

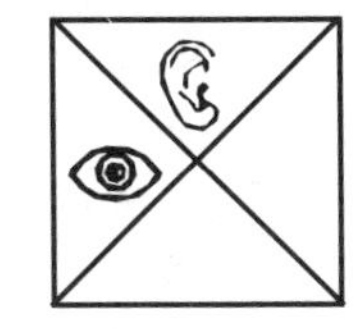

Assign a student the role of movie or literary critic. He must write a brief response to a class movie, new movie release, or reading assignment.

Newsworthy Notes

At the end of each week, select five topics that were covered that week. Divide the children into groups of four. Ask each group to write a paragraph about their assigned topic. Put the topics together to create a newspaper.

Classroom Photos

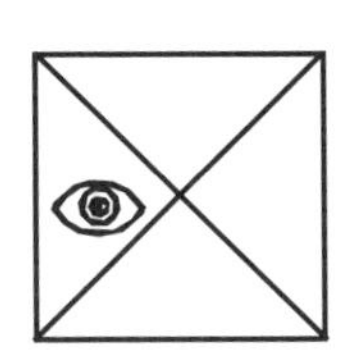

Take snapshots of students and activities in the classroom. Place the photos under the plastic coating of a photo album, and store the album where students have easy access. When a student has difficulty selecting a writing topic, encourage her to write a caption in the class album. Use wipe-off pens so you can use the same album pages again and again.

MORE Writing Responses

communication
higher-level thinking

Daily Graffiti Board

At the beginning of the year, write a question to the students on a large white board or a piece of chart paper; for example:

> "I need help planning what to do after school; can you give me some suggestions?"

Ask students to write their responses on the board. As the year progresses, encourage them to write messages to you and each other. Plan a sharing time to discuss the messages at the end of each day.

communication
motivation

Gallery Walk

Use this strategy as a review technique or to share knowledge: Hang five to seven large sheets of chart paper in the classroom or hallway. Label each piece of paper with a topic. Encourage the students to write their comments about each topic, and have them initial their responses.

Gallery Walk

MORE Writing Responses

Travels With Teddy

family involvement

This activity will involve the cooperation of each child's family and relatives. Each family needs to agree who among the relatives will "Hide Teddy" during the course of the activity.

Have each student bring a teddy bear (or another favorite stuffed animal) to school, and tell his classmates about it, including its name and where it will begin its journey. Once each student takes his bear home, the parents hide the bear with the chosen relative. The family sends postcards from the bear to the child at school, to be shared with the class. This goes on throughout the school year. At the end of the year all the bears return home from their trip, and visit the class for the last time.

If a family does not want to participate in this activity, have school personnel adopt the child's animal and send the postcards.

The family of one child in my kindergarten class included an aunt in the game; she was a flight attendant and mailed the child postcards and souvenirs from the bear from all over the world.

Class TV Guide

comprehension

Ask each student to list his favorite TV show, giving the day and time of the show, and write a brief synopsis, *TV Guide* style. Bind the pages into a book. When students cannot think of a topic to write about, give them the option of choosing a TV show.

MORE Writing Responses

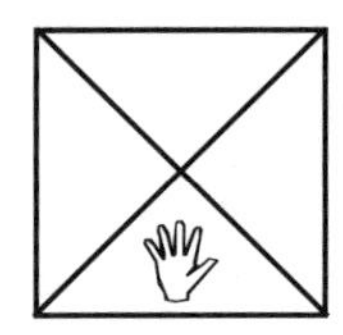

*Fan*ciful Writing

Have each student take a piece of writing paper and fold down one edge of the paper. The students each write the name of a person or thing on the first line, then pass their papers to the student behind them. These students fold another strip of the paper (in the opposite direction to begin a series of accordian folds) and write the name of a place, real or imaginary. The students pass the papers to the person on their right; the paper is folded again, and the students write a phrase about a problem each has had or has read about.

Next the students pass the papers three forward; the recipients make another fold in the papers and write the names of two more people or things. Finally, students pass the papers two forward, fold them again, and write a silly phrase.

Collect the fans, and place them in a coffee can. Each student picks one and writes a story based on all of the shared ideas.

comprehension
fluency

Written Wriddles

Use this idea to stimulate writing with less motivated writers. Glue pictures to the left inside section of several file folders. Encourage students to write riddles on the right side of the folders to describe the pictures. Pair the students and have them take turns reading the riddles to their partners and guessing what the picture is from the riddles.

MORE Writing Responses

Newsworthy Information

reading comprehension

Encourage the students to write "letters to the editor" (the teacher) at the end of each month, giving feedback and suggestions about the classroom.

Have the students write and publish articles describing topics of discussion or classroom current events.

Have students write their own advertisements for peer tutoring.

Set up a trading corner in the classroom where students can read each other's letters, stories, and advertisements.

Birdbrained Writing

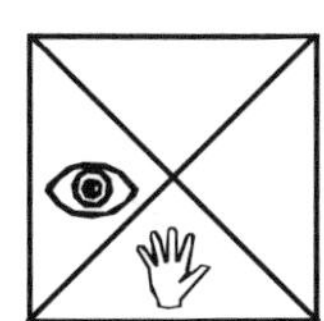

Glue single feathers onto pieces of paper (enough for each child in the class). Have the children draw or paint a picture, turning the feather into an object *other than a bird.*

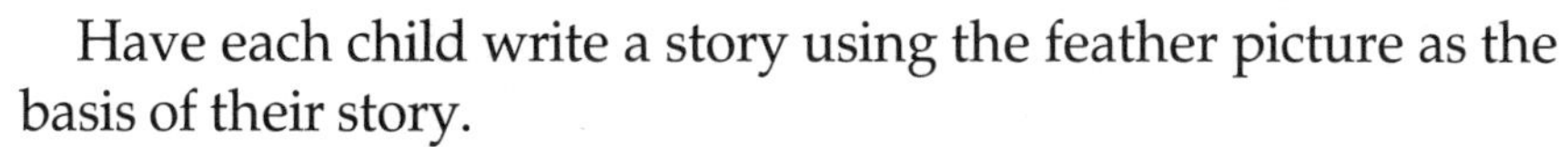

Have each child write a story using the feather picture as the basis of their story.

For variety, use Styrofoam nuggets, polished stones, and other interesting objects.

Poster Boards

Gather old posters from garage sales, other classrooms, book clubs, bookstores, or museum stores. Cut off any captions. Divide the students into groups of four and give a poster to each group. The group must create a caption for their poster. One child can do the writing, another can check the spelling, and another the punctuation. The fourth child can read the caption to the class.

Ouch! That Hurts Me!

Lessen unnecessary trips to the nurse's office with this activity. Laminate and bind a blank book cover and blank white pages. Cover the front of the book with Band Aids and gauze. Write the title, "Ouch! That Hurts Me!" on the cover. Every time a student has an ache or a pain in class, encourage him to write about his feelings in the book.

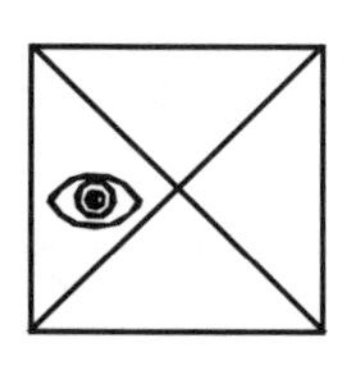

Ladder Writing

Give the students a word and have each of them write it vertically on a piece of paper.

Have students work alone or in pairs to write a sentence or poem, using each letter to begin a new phrase or verse.

If students have been working on a circus unit, their writing might look like this:

C COLORFUL, HAPPILY MY DAY BEGAN
L LAUGHING, OFF TO THE CIRCUS WE RAN
O (etc.)
W
N

Cut Ups

Find several pictures of different kinds of animals, and cut each picture into the animals' body parts. Glue body parts together to create a new creature, and display it to the students. Ask them questions about the picture, and have them write their own stories about the animal.

The Toughest Thing About Being Me

self-awareness

parental involvement

Have students write about their most difficult challenges in their diaries or journals. With their permission, place the entries on the students' desks on back-to-school night. Encourage parents to write a response in their child's journal.

Shared Pairs

relationship

communication

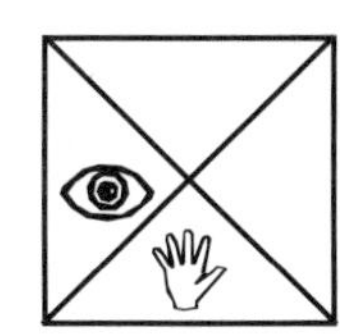

Students will eagerly participate in this activity. Make a classroom of older children in your school your partner classroom. Team each student in your class with a student "peer coach" in the other class.

Have every Friday be "Write an Entry for a Friend Day." Students write to express themselves, then collect the journals and deliver them to the other class. The children's peer coaches read the journals and write positive comments.

Daily Diary

parental involvement

Gather the class together at the end of each day. Have each student write a diary entry on a Post-It note about what he or she remembers from the day's activities. Have the students stick the notes on the door as they leave for the day; gather them, stick them on a page, and laminate them. At the end of each month, bind the daily journals. Revisit them frequently.

A side benefit of this activity is that it will help students answer the question, "What did you do in school today?" when they get home.

creative expression
comprehension
family involvement

Pizza Boxes

Collect clean, empty pizza boxes from a local pizza shop; have one for each student.

Have each child draw a picture of herself and attach it to the cover of the box. She must then write and illustrate six to eight stories representing "slices" of her life.

Use the same concept for a book review: On the outside of the box, draw a picture of the book's most memorable scene; on the inside, write and illustrate summaries of each scene to create a synopsis of the book.

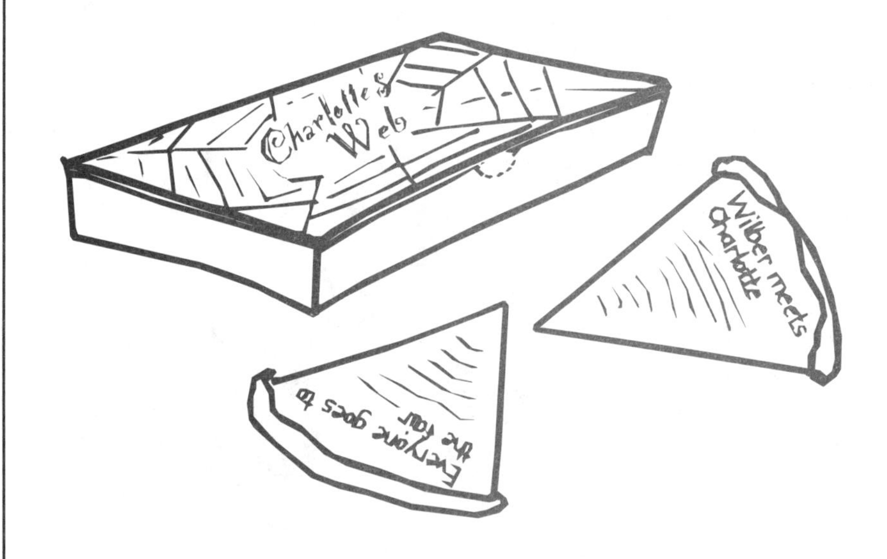

Main Idea Puzzles

Reinforce the concept of "main ideas" in writing and reading with this activity: On a piece of card stock, write a main idea or topic title. Underneath the main idea, write the supporting sentences for the topic. Cut apart the sentences, and have the students put the sentences back together to make a complete paragraph, with the main idea and supporting sentences in proper order.

comprehension
fluency

Wear a Coat
It is winter.
It might snow.
You could get wet.

Chit Chat

Cut two pictures of people or animals from magazines. Glue the pictures on a piece of paper so they face each other. Draw conversation bubbles in between the two faces. Encourage the students to create a conversation between the two people or animals by filling in the bubbles.

Say What?

Cut pictures out of magazines and catalogs that demonstrate people speaking in a variety of situations. Glue word bubbles to each picture, and laminate the pictures. Distribute them to children who have difficulty generating their own story ideas.

You can also use these pictures to review punctuation in dialogue.

Real Life

creative expression

Ask each student to bring a favorite photo to school. Display the photos in a learning center. Have students select a photo (not their own) and detail in writing what they imagine happened *before* and *after* the picture was taken.

Who's in the Beginning / Middle / End

Write ten to fifteen detailed sentences on a piece of paper. Divide each sentence into a beginning, middle, and end.

Write each part of each sentence on a separate 5" x 8" index card. Mix the cards up and distribute them to the class. On a signal, the students mingle and find the classmates with the two missing pieces of their sentence. Once they find their sentence mates, they must line up so that the parts of their sentence are in the right order.

creative expression
sequencing
punctuation

Round Robin Stories

Work in groups of five to seven. Give each student a 5" x 8" index card. Have the students each write a solid lead-in sentence for a paragraph on the card. Signal the students to pass their cards to the left. Each student reads the lead-in and writes a supporting sentence. Continue passing the cards until each child has had an opportunity to write on each card. The last child to receive the card must write the concluding sentence. Each group then chooses a team member to read the paragraphs to the class.

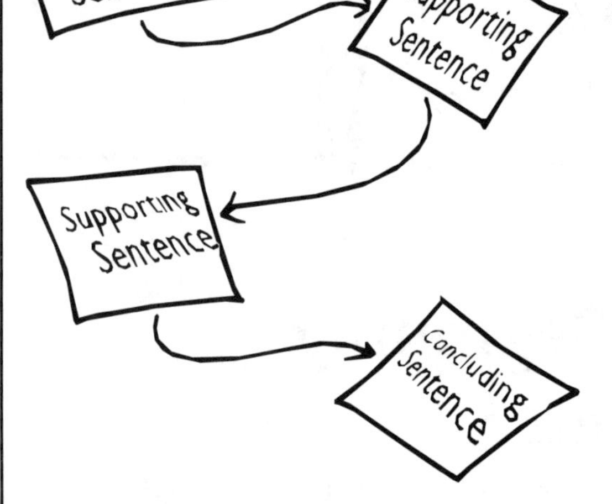

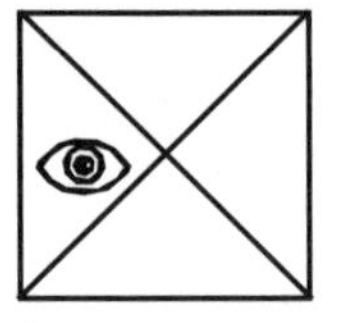

sequencing

Snowman Writing

Draw a picture of a snowman to remind children of the parts of a story: the hat is the topic, the boots are the conclusion, and all parts in between are the details in the story.

MORE Story Structure

What's the Point Here?

Cut pictures of a classroom pointer out of oak tag. On each pointer, write a variety of writing topics, and put them into a large paper bag. Have each child reach into the bag and grab a pointer. Their job is to write at least five "grabbing sentences" for each lead-in. If a child is having difficulty with his grabbing sentences, pair him off with a partner and have the pair brainstorm.

Colorful Writing

sequencing

Use sentence strips in five different colors for this activity; model the activity using a pocket chart. Write a story using the colored sentence strips as follows:

First color:	Opening of the story.
Second Color:	Building sentence.
Third Color:	Begins a second idea.
Fourth Color:	Supports or builds the second idea.
Fifth Color:	Concluding sentence.

The students use the model to write in their own journals, using colored marking pens to identify the different parts of the story.

Kite Tales

sequencing

paragraph structure

Have the students make paper kites. Write the main sentence for a paragraph on the body of each kite. Have the students write supporting sentences on the kite tails.

MORE Revising/Editing

Three Before Me

Teach students to use the cooperative learning motto, "See three before me," when editing their writing. Before a student comes to the teacher with editing questions, he must discuss editing problems with three peers, who read his work, comment on it, and initial it. (This technique can be used anytime throughout the day to help students become less dependent on the teacher.)

The End is Up

Once students have finished reading a book as a class, have them each write a new ending for the book, and share their endings with the class.

Spelling Adaptations

Post-It Spelling

blending/
letter sounds

Using the smallest Post-It tablets available, write one letter on each Post-It note for each letter of the spelling words. Give a spelling test and allow students to spell their words using the Post-It notes.

Cool Tests

writing

Have a Cool Whip test day. Have the children bring in small containers of Cool Whip. Spread the Cool Whip on top of the students' desks, and let the students write their words in it.

MORE Spelling Adaptations

blending
sequencing

Use Your Noodle

Have room mothers write letters of the alphabet on pieces of rigatoni or macaroni. Have the students use their noodles to practice stringing the spelling words.

Spell Check

Give a red card and a green card to each student. One student spells a word from the spelling list; the other students must listen. If the speller spells the word correctly, the other students hold up the green card. If the speller is wrong, they hold up the red card. Students can take turns being the spellers and checkers.

Picture This

Distribute magazines and catalogs, and have the students cut out letters and create word collages and pictures based on spelling words.

MORE Spelling Adaptations

The Great Pyramid

sequencing

Divide the students into teams. The first member from each team writes a vowel on the top of a piece of paper, then passes the paper to the teammate on his right. The teammate copies the first letter, then adds a letter to form a word. She passes the paper to the next teammate, who copies the two letters and adds another to form a three-letter word. The students continue to pass the paper, adding letters, until they can't form another word.

Tag Teams

Have the children stand in a line, and appoint one child to be the teacher's assistant. Give the assistant a spelling word on an index card. She reads the word aloud, then taps another child on the shoulder. The second child must say the first letter in the word, and wait for a nod of approval from the assistant. If he is correct, he then taps another child, who must give the second letter of the word. The children continue until they spell the word correctly.

Artful Spellers

Have the students use markers or crayons for spelling practice — the brighter and crazier they make the letters in each word, the better.

MORE Spelling Adaptations

Scrambled Eggs

Write each letter of the spelling words separately on paper eggs. Scramble the eggs and have the students "unscramble" them by spelling the words with the eggs. This is a good adaptation for students who have trouble writing words for a spelling test.

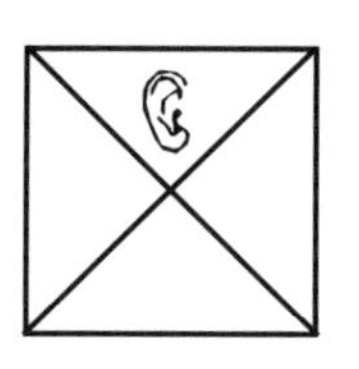

Are You?

Prepare a set of index cards with individual spelling words on them. Tell the students that you are going to play spelling detective. Have a child pick one of the cards. The other students must ask a variety of questions about the word that can be answered with "yes" or "no;" for example: "Do you have more than five letters?"; "Are you a verb?"; "Do you have an '-ing' ending?" The first student to successfully identify the spelling word chooses another card and answers questions from her classmates. Continue the game until all of the spelling words have been described.

Unscrambled List

Provide the students with a list of spelling words with the letters out of order. Their task is to unscramble the letters and spell the word correctly within a certain time frame.

For some students this activity can be used instead of writing the words during a spelling test.

The same activity can be used for vocabulary and sight words in reading.

MORE Spelling Adaptations

Bingo

sight words
decoding

Prepare a set of index cards with individual spelling words and their definitions. Make blank Bingo grids for each student. Make sure there are enough boxes on the grid for each spelling word plus the free center space. Laminate the grids. Have each student write the spelling words on his grid using wipe-off markers, placing one word randomly in each box.

Choose one student to be the caller; he reads the definition of the word, and the other students find the matching spelling word on their grids and mark it off with their markers. He continues reading definitions until someone marks off a row of words. The winning student now becomes the caller; the other students pass their cards to the student on their right, and continue playing.

Eggs Over Easy

sequencing

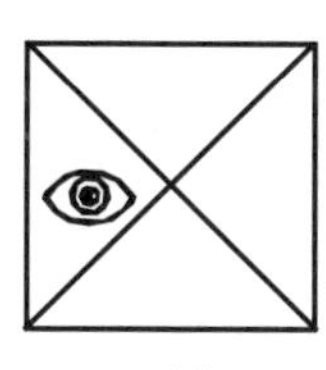

Use plastic eggs (available in toy stores around Easter time) for this activity. Scramble spelling words, write them on strips of paper, and place them inside the plastic eggs. Have a student select an egg, remove the strip of paper, and unscramble the word.

Ticket Spelling

Give each student three to five carnival tickets or raffle tickets to use in this fun spelling review. Appoint one student as the caller. The student calls out a spelling word; other students who feel they know how to spell the word hold a ticket in front of their mouths. The caller chooses one of the students to spell the word aloud; if the chosen student spells the word correctly, she puts her name on the ticket and places it in a fish bowl. She then becomes the caller. When all spelling words have been reviewed, a ticket is drawn from the fish bowl, and the student whose name is drawn wins a prize, such as a "no homework" coupon, an oral (as opposed to written) spelling test, or fifteen extra minutes with a favorite computer program.

MORE Spelling Adaptations

Rebound Spelling

Divide the students into pairs. Give one child a spelling list; she calls out a word, and her partner jumps up and down on a mini-trampoline, spelling the word letter by letter as he jumps. (If you don't have a mini-trampoline, use a jump rope.)

sight words

Spelling Spinners

Cut a large circle out of oak tag. Write the spelling words in pairs around the outside of the circle. Attach a spinner arrow to the center of the circle. Players can take turns spinning the arrow and reading the two words, then combining them into a sentence.

This activity can also be used for reading vocabulary words.

Spin Again

Create a wheel as in the above activity. Divide the circle into six or eight segments. On each segment draw or paste a picture of a spelling word. The student spins the arrow and spells the word whose picture the arrow designates.

MORE Spelling Adaptations

Spelling Word Search

Use the same format for this game as for any word search, using the week's spelling words.

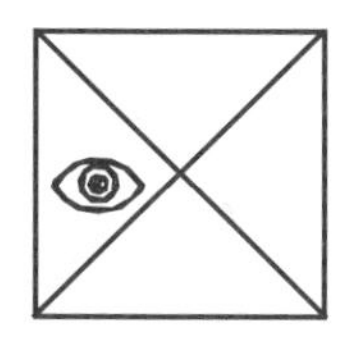

Spelling Chairs

Play this game like musical chairs: set up chairs in a line with one less chair than the number of students in the class. Tape a spelling word, face down, to the back of each chair. Play music; when the music stops, the children rush to get a chair. The child left standing calls the name of any seated student, reads the word on the chair, and asks the seated student to spell the word. If the child spells the word correctly, he gets to keep his chair, and the child left standing is out of the game. If the child who answers spells the word wrong, *he's* out of the game. One chair is removed, and the game continues.

Spelling Riddles

written expression

Have the class design riddles for each of the words in their spelling list. Place the riddles in a jar, folder, or binder. Students can pair off and take turns reading the riddles and guessing and spelling the words. Examples of riddles are:

> I am a spelling word with 6 letters.
> I am the spelling word that has one m and two t's.
> I am the word ______________.

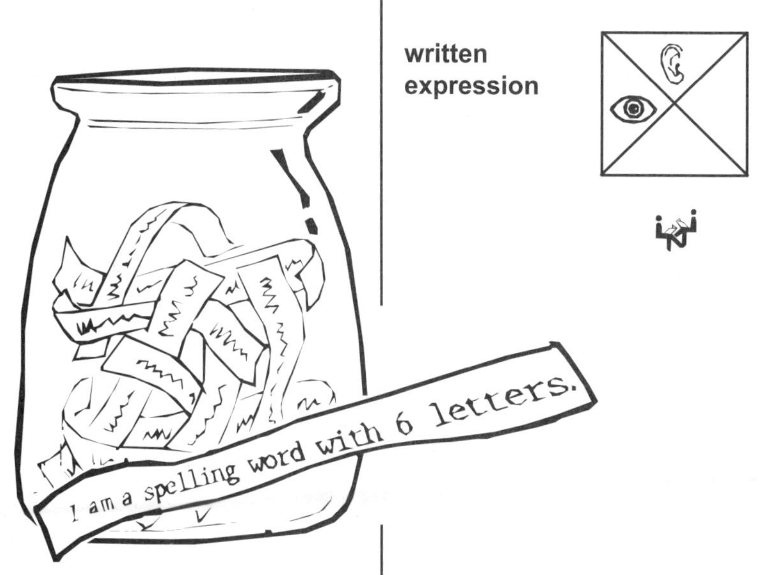

MORE Spelling Adaptations

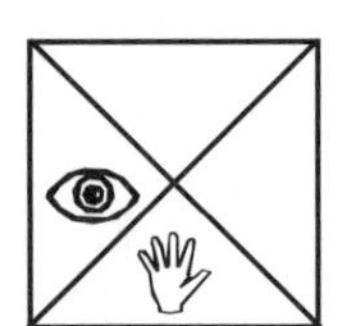

Cap-ital Letters

Before school begins, write an introductory letter to each family, asking them to save plastic caps from milk, water, or juice jugs. Print a letter of the alphabet on each cap with a permanent marking pen, and use the caps to practice spelling.

Once Upon a Time

Place a number of spelling words on the chalkboard in random fashion. Ask the students to chain the words together to make a paragraph or story.

Suspicious Spelling

Have the students work in pairs in this activity based on the game "Suspicion." Each pair has a stack of cards with spelling words written on them. The first student defines the suspicious word to his partner, who must state what the word is. If she is correct, she then spells the word, either aloud or by writing it. If she is right, she is cleared of suspicion and now becomes the detective for her partner, choosing the card, defining the word, and checking her partner's spelling.

MORE Spelling Adaptations

Spelling Context Mystery

context clues
comprehension

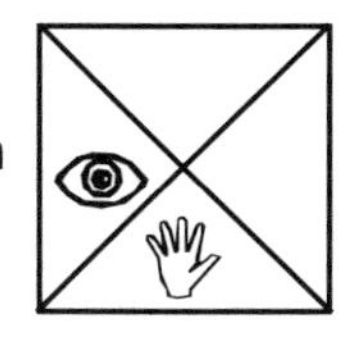

Write each spelling word on an index card. Place the cards in an envelope.

Write and number sentences on a piece of paper based on spelling words; leave blanks for the spelling words. Have the students use the context clues provided by the sentences to match the index cards to the correct sentences. Mark the appropriate sentence number on the back of each index card so students can check their own answers.

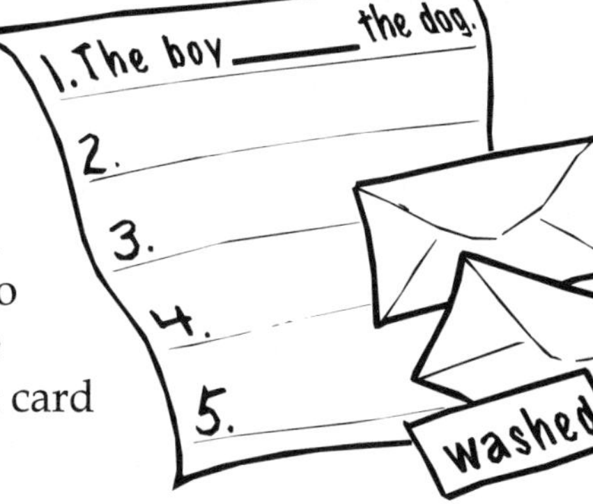

Spelling Toss

Have one student toss a Nerf Ball to a friend. The first student calls out a spelling word, and the student who caught the ball must spell the word. If the second student spells the word correctly, she tosses the ball to a third student and calls out another spelling word.

Allow struggling learners to keep spelling lists at their desks and refer to them when spelling the words.

Highlight the Words

visual
matching

For students who have difficulty writing their spelling words, have their words written for them in yellow highlighter on their test sheets. Their job is to trace the words on top of the highlighted words. This measures the students' ability to match words they hear with the correct written words, and gives them practice in writing the words.

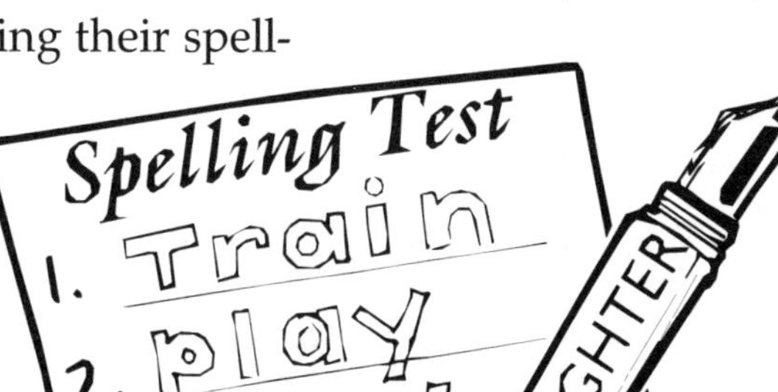

MORE Spelling Adaptations

Sensory Spelling

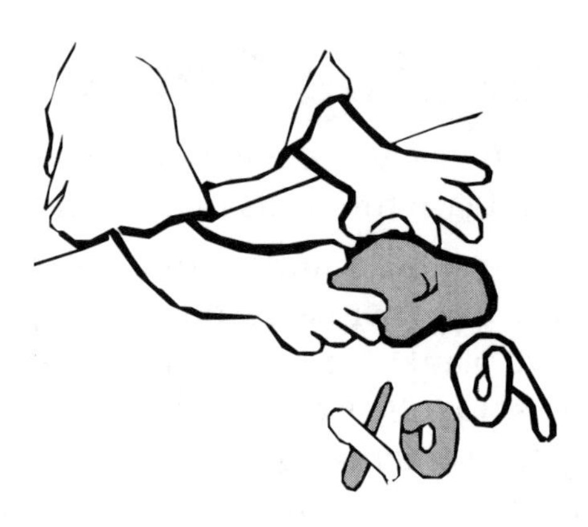

Provide students with a list of ten spelling words at a learning center. As a child reviews each word on the list, he must write the word with three different kinds of materials; for example: play dough, shaving cream, Cool Whip, a shoebox filled with salt.

memory
visual
discrimination

Right or Rong?

Write each spelling word on one half of a 5" x 8" index card. On the other half, spell the word incorrectly. Laminate the cards. The student must look at the cards and circle the correctly spelled words with a wipe-off marker.

Starts and Ends

Write the first and last letters of a spelling word on a piece of paper. Draw blanks between the two letters to represent the missing letters. Have the child fill in the missing letters.

MORE Spelling Adaptations

Spelling Charades

role play

Write each spelling word on an index card, and place the cards in a bag. Have a student select a card from the bag and dramatize the word for his classmates. The student who correctly iden-tifies the word pulls another word out of the bag and acts it out.

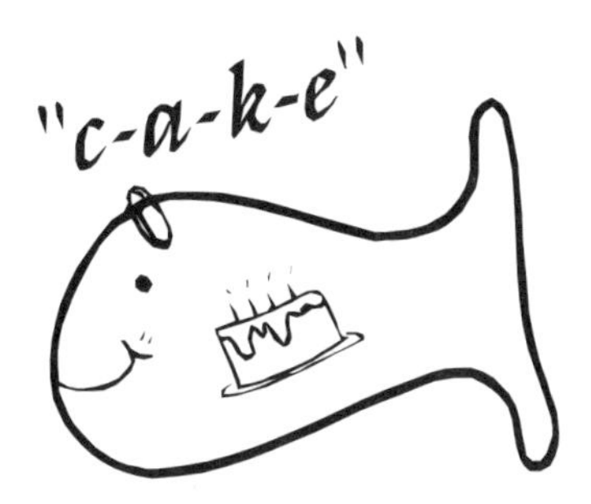

Fishing for Spelling Words

Make a fishing pole out of a stick, a piece of string, and a small magnet. Cut out a variety of oak-tag fish and laminate them. Attach a metal paper clip to each fish, along with a picture representing each spelling word. As a student catches a fish, she must spell the word that matches the picture on the fish.

Filing Cabinet Spelling Test

Select a new "special friend" each week, and permit him to take his spelling test on the teacher's filing cabinet with magnetic letters.

MORE Spelling Adaptations

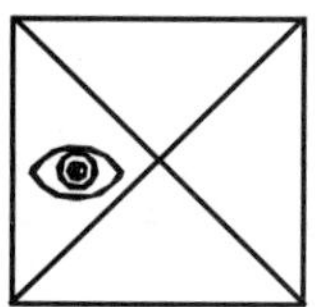

sequencing

Wheel of Fortune

Write the letters of a spelling word on individual sheets of construction paper. Tape the sheets of paper, blank side up, onto the chalkboard. Give the students a definition of the word, then have them take turns guessing which letters are in the word. As a student guesses a letter correctly, flip the paper so that the letter is visible; that student continues to guess letteers until she guesses wrong. The student who guesses what the spelling word is may put up the next word.

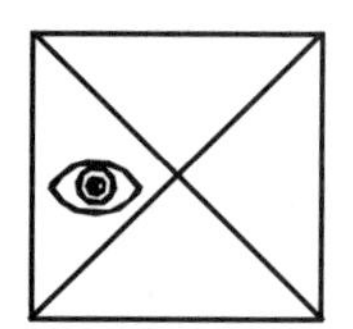

written expression

Vertical Spelling

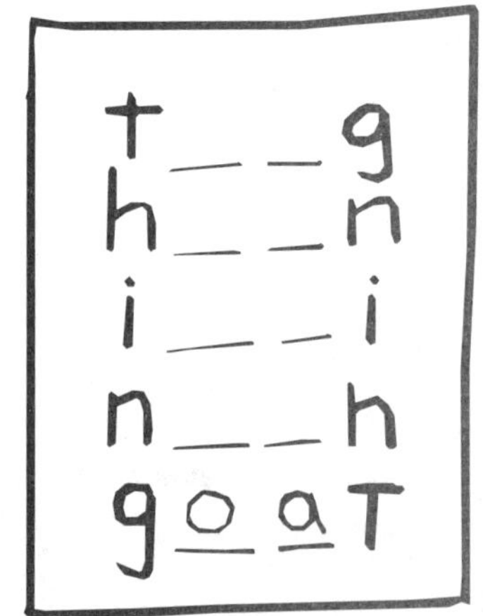

Write a spelling word vertically on the left side of a piece of paper. Now write the same word vertically on the right side, but from the bottom up. Students try to create new words by writing letters between the two vertical words.

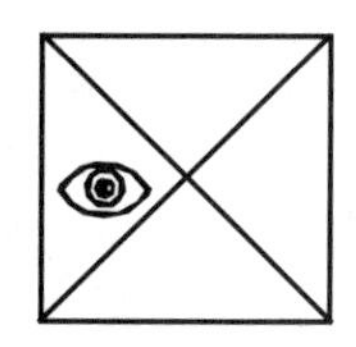

written expression

Hee-Haw

Give the students a list of spelling words. Challenge the students to combine two or more words from the list to make a silly sentence.

MORE Spelling Adaptations

Spell It

definition

Select a word from the spelling list. Instead of dictating the word to the child, give a definition of the word. For example:

"Spell me the word that is a two-wheeled vehicle you ride." (bike)

Opposites

sequencing

comprehension

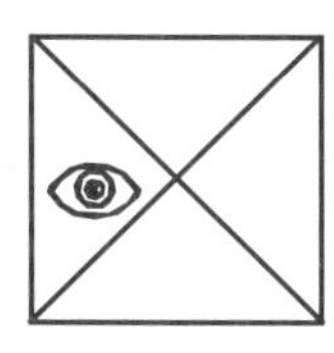

Have the students use each of their spelling words in a sentence, and string the sentences together to form a story. After completing this task, have them go back to the beginning and replace each spelling word with its opposite. Watch what happens to the storyline.

Sticker Spelling

Purchase sets of letter stickers. Give each student a page of letters. Instruct the students to use the stickers for spelling tests rather than writing the words with pencil and paper.

MORE Spelling Adaptations

Funny Buck Test

Contract each child for a specific score on her spelling test. Some children will aim for 100 percent, others for 75 to 90 percent. Each week the student reaches her goal, she receives a one-dollar "funny buck" (see page 72). At the end of each marking period, throw a class yard sale; students can use their funny bucks to purchase items at the sale.

sequencing

Chips-Ahoy

Write letters on one side of individual Bingo chips; make sure you have enough of each letter to spell all the words in the current spelling list. Place the Bingo chips in a coffee can; have the child shake the chips out of the can and spell the words. Some children may need to work from a word list.

In the Doghouse

Use this activity to review long and short vowel sounds in spelling words. Cut out two separate doghouses. Label one house "long vowel," and the other "short vowel." Cut out a variety of dog shapes, and write a spelling word on each dog. The child must put each dog in the correct house according to the vowel sounds. Write the answers on the backs of the dogs for self-checking.

Laminate the dogs for reuse before you write the words on them.

MORE Spelling Adaptations

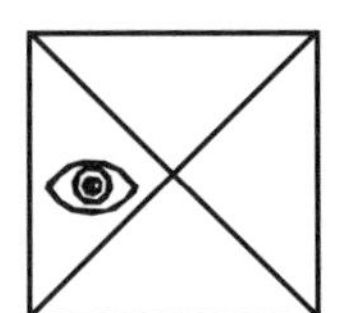

adjectives
adverbs

Pyramid Activity

Draw boxes in the form of a pyramid. Write a spelling word in the top box. Have the students copy the word, then add an adjective, in the second set of boxes, then add another adjective or adverb onto the phrase in the third set of boxes. The adjectives and adverbs must fit into the boxes given.

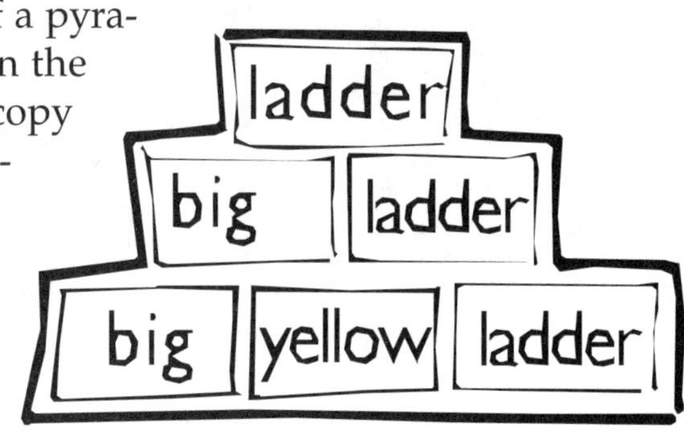

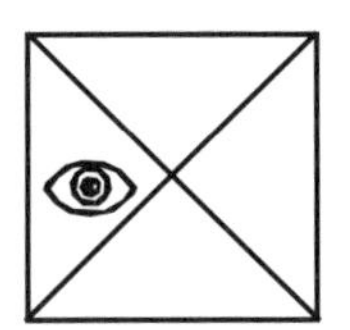

dictionary
skills

Spelling Crosswords

Create a blank crossword grid for the week's spelling words, and write a definition for each word. The student must use the definitions to fill in the crossword puzzle. Some students may find a word bank helpful for this activity.

Spelling Scrabble

Use a set of letter tiles or handmade letter squares for this activity. Place enough letters to spell all the words in the spelling list in a Ziploc bag. Have the children work in pairs; the students each pull five letters from the bag and take turns trying to spell a word from the spelling list. If a student can't spell one of the spelling words using the first five letters, he may discard one of the letters (by putting it back into the bag) and pull another letter from the bag. If he still can't spell a word, his partner gets a turn. The students take turns pulling and discarding letters until all the words have been spelled.

MORE Spelling Adaptations

3-D Spelling

Write each spelling word on a separate index card. Give the children foam letters, and have them spell each word using the foam letter underneath the word on the index card. For more of a tactile experience, have the children trace the foam letters with their fingers.

You may also dictate the words to the students and have them form them with the foam letters.

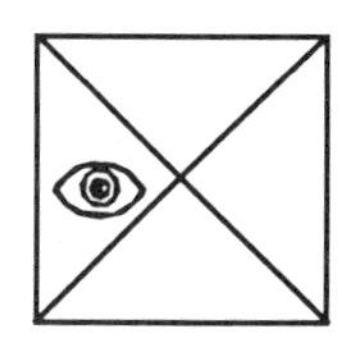

Create a set of laminated oak-tag gingerbread cookies for this activity, and write a spelling word on each cookie. Appoint one child to be "it." This child chooses a cookie and gives a definition for the word on the cookie; for instance: "I have a spelling word that means 'to help'." He chooses another child to give the correct word: "assist." If the second child guesses the right word, the student who is "it" asks him to spell the word. If the word is spelled correctly, the student earns the cookie.

This game can be adapted for some struggling learners by having the speller give the first and last letters of the word.

Color Word Review

sequencing

Use an Ellison die machine or letter stencils for this activity. Cut out letters of color words in paper of the corresponding color. Place all of the letters in a coffee can. Have the child empty the can and assemble the words by color and letters.

red

blue

MORE Spelling Adaptations

String Spellers

Write letters on a variety of large and small beads. Instead of having the children take written spelling tests, have them spell the words by stringing the beads.

This adaptation works especially well when the spelling tests are developed around word families, and only the initial letter has to be switched.

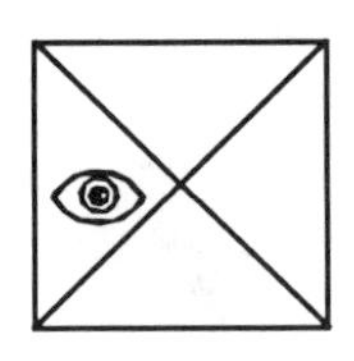

written expression

Box 'em Up

Continue to review spelling words after the week in which they are assigned. At the end of each week, write the words from the spelling test on individual index cards, and place the cards in a decorated box. The number of words in the box will increase from week to week.

Have a student select one word each day from the box. This student must try to find the word while reading, and use the word in writing, throughout the day.

Spelling Scrabble

Place old scrabble letters or individual letter squares in a container; make sure the container is opaque so that the children cannot see the letters. Write each spelling word to be reviewed on individual sentence strips. Give each child a sentence strip; the child must pull one letter from the container. If the child can use the letter to spell the word on her strip, she can keep the letter; if not, she discards the letter. Keep passing the container around the class, allowing each child to pull one letter at a time, and see who can build her word first.

Use this activity with individual students instead of a written spelling test.

Parent Pages

This section gives you ideas for communicating with parents, and includes pages that you can copy and either give to your students, or send home for parents. Some of the pages contain general information useful for parents of all elementary school children; others are suitable for specific grade levels.

One idea is to create a four-page newsletter using pages 163-165 and adding either page 166, 167 or 168, depending on the grade level of your class.

Contents:

Helping Me Read

Dear ______________________________,

My teacher, ______________________, gave me this book to bring home tonight. I want you to listen to me read the book.

If I come to a word I do not know, remind me to look at the letters in the word, to look at the rest of the sentence, and to sound out the word. I might need to make a good guess about what that word is. It makes me feel good if you let me try to figure out unknown words on my own.

Sometimes we can take turns reading different pages in the book. Just spending quality time with you makes me happy.

At the end of our reading time together it makes me proud to hear you say what a good job I have done. You can even ask me some questions about the story we read, just to see what I can remember. I need to take the book back to school tomorrow in this same big envelope.

Thank you for helping me.

Love,

Important Message

Dear Room _______ Families:

Here are the classroom rules and consequences your child and I have developed. These rules and consequences will help us create a classroom where every child can make wise choices about behavior. The students will then be able to learn in a positive, nurturing classroom environment. The plan below outlines our rules, rewards and consequences. Please review these expectations with your child and sign on the dotted line. Return this to school and I will send home a copy for your files.

To encourage students to follow these rules, I will support behavior with Happygrams, rewards, and privileges.

Rules

1. Follow directions.
2. One person speaks at a time.
3. Keep your hands and feet to yourself.
4. Use inside voices.
5. Treat others kindly.

If your child makes a choice to break a rule, the following steps will be taken:

First consequence:	A silent, nonverbal warning.
Second consequence:	A verbal reminder.
Third consequence:	Time out in the thinking chair.
Fourth consequence:	Visit to the principal and phone call home.

- -

I have read these rules and expectations with my child and will support the classroom teacher.

____

(parent's signature)

I understand what is expected of me in school.

____

(child's signature)

Open communication makes learning time productive time.

Top Banana!

Date: ________________

Dear Family,

Your child, ____________________, has been selected to be the focus of the Top Banana Friend in Room _____ next week. Please help all of us celebrate the specialness of your child by providing the following items for our classroom bulletin board:

A recent photograph of your child.

A photograph of your child's family.

Any additional baby/young pictures of your child that would help us see how unique your child is.

Also, please fill out the following section and return it to school with your child on Monday. Congratulations for having a Top Banana in your house.

- -

I live at ______________________________.

My favorite things to do alone are ____________________.

My favorite things to do with my family are _____________________.

What my family likes best about me are ___________________.

Three words my family would use to describe me are ______________,

______________, and ______________.

My favorite food is ____________________________.

What I want to do when I grow up: ___________________.

Please remember that each Friday the Top Banana is encouraged to bring anyone from home to share in Chart Time. You are encouraged to bring any family members to this special time, including pets. Feel free to stay for lunch, but your pet can't be included in that.

Announcing a New Unit!

Dear families,

Next week we will be starting a unit on ____________________.
This unit will include many different aspects of __________________.
My main goal for teaching the children about this is ________________

____

At school throughout the unit we will:

1.

2.

3.

4.

At home you can support this unit by:

1.

2.

3.

Special events, assemblies, and field trips will include:

1.

2.

Call me at ______________________________ if you have anything you can contribute to this unit of study.

Create a Newsletter!

Instead of sending a lot of miscellaneous notes home, organize your communications with parents by creating an informative weekly newsletter.

ROOM 202 NEWS

Tap and Tell

We had a wonderful week this week. Ask your child how we played Tap and Tell to help us learn more about each other.

$$$$$$$$$$

If you have not sent in your snack money for the month, please send it in Monday. You may send a check or cash. The September amount is $10.00.

School Daze

Back-to-School Night is scheduled for September 25.

The building will be open from 6:00 PM to 8:00 PM. This is a wonderful time to bring your child to school and share our classroom. See you then!

Clapping Match

Ask your child to show you how we do clapping patterns in the K-1 room. Have your child teach you how we do this and when we use it. This not only helps with auditory memory but with self-control as well. Try it at home.

Funny Bunny

Aimee Stopper has Thumper this weekend. The bunny, as well as Thumper's diary, will go home with Aimee and her family. Who will get Thumper next week?

Letter Land

The letter of the week is Jj. Help your child place a J item in the letter bag. Send a J snack on Friday.

J

How Can I Help My Child at Home?

Parents frequently ask the question, "What can I do at home to help my child at school?" Here are some suggestions:

1. Give high priority to school attendance.

When a student is absent or tardy, it is impossible to recreate the many learning opportunities that occurred throughout the day. Yes, worksheets and textbooks can be sent home, and that work is important, but the classroom interaction cannot be replaced.

2. Know what your child is studying in school.

Knowing what the class is studying gives you the opportunity to be on the alert for complementary events and activities such as visiting a historic site, watching a related movie or TV show, finding a book on the subject, visiting a library, or talking with an expert. It is also helpful if you can find ways for your child to practice school skills in real-life situations.

3. Have a regularly scheduled time for homework.

Each evening a student should spend some time with schoolwork: completing written assignments, reviewing notes from the day's classes, reading a good book, working on long-term assignments, studying in advance for tests, etc. While there are many activities competing for a child's time and commitment, schoolwork should always be part of the schedule. Help your child learn how to prioritize assignments and divide up the available time. Decide which assignments to do first. Is it best to do the favorite first or to get the least favorite out of the way? Should the written assignments be done first or should the reading come first? Is the assignment due tomorrow or are there several more days to work on that assignment? Is this something that can be done independently or is help needed?

5. Provide a homework box.

This box will contain the supplies necessary for typical homework, such as pencils, scissors, glue, paper, a ruler, colored pencils, etc. Having such supplies readily available reduces lost time and energy getting ready to do homework.

6. Help your child prepare for tests.

While some studying can be done independently, it is usually helpful to have a partner quiz the child with questions taken from the notes and/or text. Sometimes it is beneficial to make flashcards, create lists, draw pictures, or make up sayings to highlight important information, create mental pictures, and/or tell someone else what you learned or how to do the process. Learning is often a social event. Take some time each night to review.

It is also helpful if you can find ways for your child to practice school skills in real-life situations.

continued next page

7. Look for opportunities for quick rehearsals.

Remember the questions that seemed especially troublesome, the word that was hardest to spell, or the math fact that was most difficult to remember. Give a quick quiz in the car, while waiting in line, while waiting for the toaster to pop, or any other time when a few minutes become available. Frequent short practices can sometimes be more helpful than one long session.

8. Focus on learning rather than grades.

While grades are an indicator of learning, they should not be the goal. Students should study for what they learn, not for a grade. Some students have an inordinate fear of making mistakes or being less than perfect. Turn mistakes into opportunities for problem solving. Focus on what can be learned from a mistake and how to improve the next time. Remember the old saying, "The man who never made a mistake never did anything." It is important, however, not to make the same mistake over and over again.

9. Be a cheerleader.

In a study at Teachers College, Columbia University, families were videotaped helping their students with homework. It was found that parents who act as cheerleaders raise confident kids who are able to tackle even the most difficult homework assignments. Say something like, "Sure this is hard, but I know you've done work this hard before. Now let's stop and look at the problem again."

10. Remember to maintain a balance.

Children need variety. They need a balance between work and play; a balance between scheduled activities and time to relax; a balance between time with friends and time to be alone. Listen to the needs and wants of your child.

If your child spends an excessive amount of time on homework, complains that school is too hard, repeatedly has difficulty with assignments or tests, or wants to stay home despite no physical symptoms of illness, call the teacher or write a note. It may be time to brainstorm collaboratively the source of the problem and the potential solutions. A partnership between home and school is vital to a child's success.

Homework Helpers

- Have adequate supplies ready for the child.
- Your child might need daily reminders regarding homework. Schedule a specific time for your child to be working. Have a quiet area, not necessarily a desk. A kitchen table, counter top, or small table in a bedroom would work. If your child has no work to do, have the child sit at that designated space and silently read.
- Have all of your children do their homework at the same time; this will free you to assist on an as-needed basis.
- Learn to genuinely praise your child. Be certain to give praise about an act your child accomplished rather than a physical trait.
- Check your child's assignment book daily and initial it. This keeps the teacher informed of how often you review your child's work.

Helping Your Child Become a Better Reader

Children change from learning to read to reading to learn as they improve their reading skills. Here are some tips that might help you help your child become a successful reader. Keep in mind that comprehending what is read is a cornerstone for success in all subject areas.

1. Read to your child.

No matter how old your child is, children love to be read to. Even when my daughter was in Junior High School I would read to her at night. Perhaps it was a study assignment or just the fact that we both cherished the quiet times, but reading can be a wonderful bonding session. If your child is young, read a book that is on your child's level of understanding. Discuss the pictures and begin to notice some words. Try to read slowly and clearly and ask questions as you go along.

2. Hear your child read to you.

Many times children enjoy reading a page to you and then hearing you read the next page. Some children choose to read a paragraph and then have Mom or Dad read the next paragraph to them. Talk with your child about reading fluently and reading with expression. Sometimes tape recording the child helps with both fluency and expression.

3. Share ideas.

Ask your child questions about what was read or heard. Ask general questions and then build into more specific questions. Draw pictures about comprehension. Write reviews about chapters and books.

4. Don't punish with literacy.

Try to never punish a child with reading: "You didn't listen or behave . . . so go to your room and read."

Create a Homework Kit!

Create this survival kit for your child to use when doing homework.

Grades K-2: Crayons, glue sticks, markers, pencils, erasers, colored paper, white paper, lined paper, hole punch, stapler, scissors (try Friskers), assignment folder, assignment calendar.

Grades 3-5: Pencils, pens, dictionary, atlas, paper, colored pens and pencils, glue sticks, hole punch, stapler, paper clips, erasers, index cards, homework hotline phone number, books, and books on tape, tape recorder.

Tip: Even if your child has no homework on a particular day, urge him or her to read independently for an hour or so in his or her usual study area. This will help your child learn to create and follow a set schedule.

Make sure you praise your child for his or her accomplishments rather than physical abilities. "I loved how you sat right down tonight and worked on that spelling paper without any reminders from Daddy and me," rather than, "I am so proud of how your hair looks."

Try to praise your child in front of other adults to help them see how sincere you are.

Help Your Kindergartener Be Independent

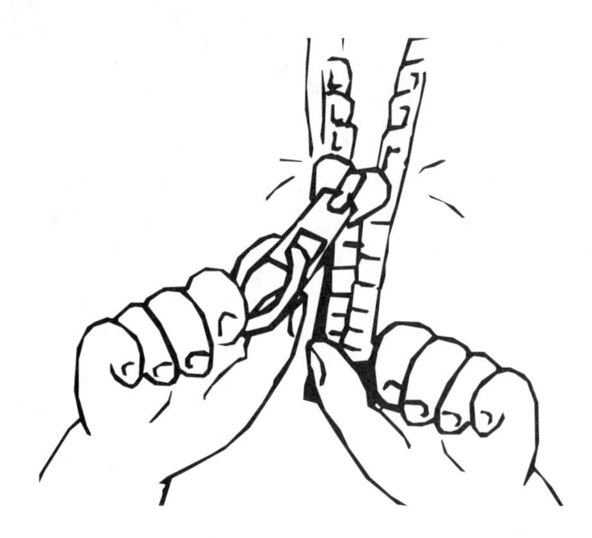

1. Can your child open and close all clothes fasteners?
2. Can your child zip and unzip his or her coat easily? If not, attach a large key ring to the zipper pull to make it easier.
3. Is your child able to buckle and tie shoes? If not, try Velcro shoes or laces that never need to be tied.
4. Can your child put on his or her boots? If not, try slipping feet into plastic bags, then putting on the boots.
5. Remember, one-piece jumpsuits have to come off completely at bathroom breaks; many children cannot handle this.
6. One-piece body suits worn under jumpers or skirts need to be removed completely as well.
7. Do all coats or sweaters have a loop to use for hanging them?
8. Is your child's classroom too hot or too cold for his or her new clothes?
9. Make sure coats, jackets, and backpacks do not have any hanging loops or ties that could get caught in a bus door.
10. Can your child manage a backpack independently?

On the Road to SUCCESS

1. Getting Organized

You will need:

- three-ring binder (2")
- pencils (sharpened)
- colored pencils
- erasers
- highlighter

How do I keep track of assignments?

Copy assignments for each subject in the assignment book (provided by the school).

Where do I put loose papers?

Assign a section of your binder to a certain subject.

How can I keep by binder neat?

Always put your papers away in the proper place.

How can I remember to bring my assignments to school?

Pack up all schoolwork before bedtime.

2. Studying for Tests

- Review notes daily.
- Make vocabulary flash cards.
- Write possible test question and answers.
- Study with a classmate, brother, sister, or parent.
- Make a study guide.
- Keep an up-to-date, completed notebook.
- Punch holes in your loose papers and put them into the appropriate section or your binder.

3. Preparing for Projects

1. Use a planning guide.
2. Mark due dates on your calendar.
3. Follow the teacher's guidelines.
4. Gather supplies early.
5. Add color and drawings to your project.
6. Use pens and markers for final projects.

4. Completing Homework

What is homework?

Homework provides practice of concepts and skills presented in class. It could include a review of notes, completing work-sheets, writing, and reading.

Where shall I do it?

Choose a quiet area at home.

What do I need?

A Homework Box could include:

sharpened pencils
erasers
highlighter markers
colored pencils
paper
scissors
ruler
index cards

How much homework will I have?

Expect about a half hour every day.

How often will I have homework?

Usually homework is assigned every day.

Why do I have homework?

Homework should help you learn and understand concepts covered in school.

What if I miss class?

In the event of absences, a homework partner of your choice can collect assignments for you. A conference with your teacher will help you understand a missed concept.

5. Getting Help

Student:

- Ask the teacher questions.
- Ask the teacher for extra help.
- Talk to the guidance counselor.
- Make an appointment for a conference with the teacher.

Parent:

- Call your child's teacher at school.
- Make an appointment for a conference with the teacher and/or guidance counselor.

What Does It Take to Be a Good Student?

How can I be responsible?

- Keep a calendar.
- Complete work on time.
- Have the supplies I need.
- Have a homework buddy.
- Ask for help when I need it.
- Plan ahead.

What are study skills?

- Being prepared every day.
- Studying ahead; studying for a test requires several days of preparation.
- Using flash cards.
- Studying with a buddy.
- Making up my own questions.
- Reviewing quiz questions before a test.
- Doing practice problems.
- Reviewing notes daily.

What are organization skills?

Keep an Agenda

- update daily
- take to each class
- keep in notebook
- list all assignments even if completed
- check off as each is finished

Put Together a Notebook

- 3-ring, 2 inch-depth best
- dividers for each subject
- keep papers in order
- fasten all papers in notebook
- use notebook pencil case
- have a pocket for papers to be signed

Do Your Homework

- set aside a time for homework
- make a homework box

pencils	pens
eraser	ruler
scissors	calculator
highlighter	glue
colored pencils	tape
white paper	
reinforcements	

- check and re-check work
- check assignment in calendar
- make neatness a priority
- pack bookbag before bedtime

How much homework will I have?

Plan to spend one hour every night on school work.

Will I ever have more than one hour of homework?

Occasionally, but you may also sometimes have less.

If I am absent, what do I do about my homework?

- You are responsible for getting your homework from your buddy.
- If possible, homework should be completed on time.
- If needed, extra time will be given equal to the days absent.
- Tests and quizzes should be made up quickly.

How should I communicate with my teacher?

- Ask for help politely if directions are not clear.
- Talk to the teacher: before school, before class, after class, during recess, or after school.
- Talk to the teacher be fore a little problem becomes a BIG problem.
- Don't be shy . . . no problem is too small.

For parents:

"How can I help my child?"

- Start your child's day off with a good breakfast.
- Insist on a special time for homework.
- Help your child assemble a homework box.
- Check calendar daily.
- Make sure bookbag is packed before bedtime.
- Communicate with the teacher as soon as a question arises.
- Encourage responsibility in your child.
- Help your child develop study skills.

Tickets to Success

Please feel free to cut these tickets apart and return them to school with your child's homework.

I have seen my child's completed homework.

My child and I worked together to complete this work.

This homework was done independently and my child kept it private.

This product was proudly inspected by ____________________ on the home front.

We are so proud of ____________________ for completing this homework in a timely fashion.

Parent activities for summer

JUNE

Sunday	Monday	Tuesday	Wednesday	Thursday	Friday	Saturday
		Look in a mirror; name and move different body parts. 1	Fingerpaint with chocolate pudding — yummy. 2	Catch fireflies in a plastic jar. Count them. 3	Find and count anything red that can move in your house. 4	Cook with a grownup. Tell what you did first, next, and last. 5
Enjoy a quiet family activity. 6	Say some nursery rhymes. Act one out. 7	Make and wrap sandwiches for a family picnic. 8	Make a diamond, square and rectangle using straws or toothpicks. 9	Make a tent with a blanket and chairs. Give directions to move inside, next to, beside, etc. 10	Name as many fruits and vegetables as you can at the grocery store or market. 11	Practice buttoning, snapping and zipping your coat and other clothes. 12
Put a puzzle together as a family. 13	Help wash the car. 14	Think of a new way to play with an old toy. 15	Can you find something that is rough, smooth, wet, and dry? 16	Name and find two things that could become both hot and cold. 17	Make a picture using cereal and macaroni. Glue it on a paper plate. 18	Have someone read you your favorite story. Act out a special part. 19
Sweep the sidewalk. Pick two yellow flowers. 20	Go outside and name two things that are high and low. Draw a picture of something low. 21	Play Simon Says by touching body parts named. 22	Taste something sweet, sour, and salty. 23	Play a guessing game. Put out six objects. Take away one and describe what is missing. 24	Help match socks in the laundry basket. 25	Sort buttons, screws, and nails in empty muffin tins. 26
Listen to a story on tape. Draw a picture of the main character. 27	List three things that you plan to do tomorrow. 28	Draw a picture of your family. Label the members. 29	Visit the public library. Choose three books that you can take home to read later. 30			

Professional Bibliography

Dubelle, Stanley T., and Hoffman, Carol M. *Misbehavin' I and II.* Lancaster, PA: Technomic Publishing Co., 1984 and 1986.

Dunn, Rita, and Dunn, Kenneth. "Kids Must Learn How to Learn Alone." *Phi Delta Kappan,* March 1987.

Feldman, Jean R. *Wonderful Rooms Where Children Can Bloom! Over 500 Innovative Ideas and Activities for Your Child-Centered Classroom.* Peterborough, NH: Crystal Springs Books, 1997.

Goodman, Gretchen. *Inclusive Classrooms From A to Z: A Handbook for Educators.* Columbus, OH: Teachers' Publishing Group, 1994.

———. *I Can Learn! Strategies and Activities for Gray-Area Children.* Peterborough, NH: Crystal Springs Books, 1995.

Grant, Jim. *A Common Sense Guide to Multiage Practices.* Columbus, OH: Teachers Publishing Group, 1994.

Greene, Lawrence J. *Kids Who Underachieve.* New York: Simon & Schuster, 1989.

Hoffman, Carol. *Reaching and Teaching the Kids Today.* Rosemont, NJ: Modern Learning Press, 1996.

Ingraham, Phoebe Bell. *Creating and Managing Learning Centers: A Thematic Approach.* Peterborough, NH: Crystal Springs Books, 1997.

Pavelka, Patricia. *Making the Connection: Learning Skills Through Literature (K-2).* Peterborough, NH: Crystal Springs Books, 1996.

———. *Making the Connection: Learning Skills Through Literature (3-6).* Peterborough, NH: Crystal Springs Books, 1997.

Vail, Priscilla. *Learning Styles.* Rosemont, NJ: Modern Learning Press, 1994.

Bedtime stories